SO LETS HEAR THE APPLAUSE

The Story of the Jewish Entertainer

Also by Michael Freedland

AL JOLSON
IRVING BERLIN
JAMES CAGNEY
FRED ASTAIRE
SOPHIE: THE SOPHIE TUCKER STORY
JEROME KERN
ERROL FLYNN (in the USA: THE TWO LIVES OF ERROL FLYNN)
GREGORY PECK
MAURICE CHEVALIER
PETER O'TOOLE
THE WARNER BROTHERS
KATHARINE HEPBURN

and with Morecambe and Wise

THERE'S NO ANSWER TO THAT

SO LETS HEAR THE APPLAUSE

The Story of the Jewish Entertainer

MICHAEL FREEDLAND

Illustrated by
TOPOL

For Carol
with lots of applause

Michael Freedland

1985.

VALLENTINE, MITCHELL

First published 1984 in Great Britain by
VALLENTINE MITCHELL AND COMPANY LIMITED
Gainsborough House, 11 Gainsborough Road,
London E11 1RS, England

and in the United States of America by
VALLENTINE MITCHELL AND COMPANY LIMITED
c/o Biblio Distribution Centre
81 Adams Drive, P.O. Box 327, Totawa, N.J. 07511

Copyright © 1984 Michael Freedland

British Library Cataloguing in Publication Data

Freedland, Michael
   So lets hear the applause.
   1. Jewish entertainers
   I. Title
   790.2'092'2   PN1584

   ISBN 0-85303-215-7

Printed and bound in Great Britain by
T. J. Press (Padstow) Ltd., Padstow, Cornwall

FOR JONATHAN

בֵּן חָכָם יְשַׂמַּח־אָב

A wise son maketh a
glad father ...
(Proverbs 10:1)

Contents

Prologue

So what is an entertainer?

In the context of this book he (or she) is a person who does more than just sing, act or perform conjuring tricks, though he may of course do those things as well. He becomes an entertainer – or perhaps a great entertainer, for all the people in this book are that – when he in some way achieves an influence on the audience; a person whose very magnetism reaches over the footlights, from the screen or even from a page of sheet music, and makes the members of that audience feel as though they're part of the act themselves. Which indeed they are.

Writing a book about Jewish entertainers is rather like producing one on black athletes. Everyone knows the incredible contribution they have made to their profession, but what more is there to say?

Firstly – and simply – this is a story never chronicled before in one volume and one which deserves some sort of detailed attention. Second, this is not intended as a final definitive work, in which every possible question is answered, every gap in people's general show-biz knowledge filled in. I shall be content if it merely prompts people to ask why some facts were omitted and equally why certain names were given prominence while others were ignored.

What I will say is that this is intended as a subjective look at what was undoubtedly a phenomenon. The opinions are mine, the names are the ones I think deserve mention.

The question I am certain I will be most frequently asked is: "How did you choose the order in which you placed the individual character studies?" Some names are easier to position – and to justify their place – than are others.

So Lets Hear The Applause

Al Jolson is number one in this book because he is still remembered as the World's Greatest Entertainer – he also happened to be Jewish. The Marx Brothers, as the dominant figures in screen comedy and so much of American humour besides, would be the first had there been no Al Jolson. Sophie Tucker I have selected because, among Jewish entertainers, it would be hard to find anyone with a stronger hold on the heart and affections of Jewish audiences. If she was no Al Jolson – and for that matter no Judy Garland (and I mention her so early on to confound any suggestion that I think the Jews were the *only* great entertainers) – her place as a *heimishe* favourite is assured. The order I have chosen for her and the others is meaningless, a mere juggling act, a simple shuffling of the pack.

This has been very much a labour of love, conceived over a very long time. It was helped on its way enormously by the kind co-operation of people like the late Jack Benny, Edward G.Robinson, George Jessel and the very-much-still-with-us-George Burns, as well as Chaim Topol, whose delightful illustrations form so important a part of this book, Larry Adler, Ron Moody, Frankie Vaughan, Sammy Cahn, Walter Matthau and Joel Grey, all of whom granted me interviews either specifically for this book or on previous occasions. Ted Shapiro provided most of the detail for the chapter on Sophie Tucker – as he did for my previous biography of Sophie – and for much background on the whole era. I must thank, too, the librarians of the Lincoln Centre, New York, for their superb help and the Academy of Motion Picture Arts and Sciences, Beverly Hills.

MICHAEL FREEDLAND

There's No Business Like Show Business

There is something strangely paradoxical about the theme of the Jewish entertainer. On the one hand, there is not the slightest doubt thát in America – and in Europe at various times too – the Jewish contribution to show business has been immense. But it is equally true that there are few other businesses where a person's origins have mattered less.

It was Al Jolson – who despite his black-face make-up was probably the most Jewish entertainer of them all – who said on a war-time show: "My dream is to make the world as democratic as the theatre. It's a place where a guy's race, religion or colour just doesn't matter."

It was *schmaltzy* – incidentally, one of the literally hundreds of Yiddish words that have crept into general usage via the theatre – but it was also essentially true.

Adolf Hitler and his henchmen Goebbels and Rosenberg tried often enough to publish photographs of world-renowned Jewish entertainers in the hope they would provoke further anti-Semitism outside Germany. But although films containing Jewish actors were banned in the Nazi-dominated countries and the entertainers concerned were unable to play on German stages or in Occupied Europe, the effect elsewhere was almost non-existent. Members of Sir Oswald Mosley's British Union of Fascists ended a thoroughly enjoyable day of Jew-baiting in London's East End by swooning over Leslie Howard (born Stainer) in *Pygmalion*. In the United States there was nothing inconsistent in belonging to the American Nazi Bund and laughing at Eddie Cantor.

It is also true that some rather less talented performers blamed the Jewish "stranglehold" on the theatre for their failure to make it in what was known as the "big time". I can remember meeting an 80-year-old veteran of the "two-a-day"

1

(two performances a day, in other words vaudeville) sitting in the New York Lambs Club and saying that the reason he had never made it was "because I belonged to the wrong religion".

Yet since he had grown up in the days when the American musical stage was dominated by a white Anglo-Saxon Protestant called Charles Dillingham, an Irish Catholic named George M. Cohan and a Protestant of Dutch ancestry known as Florenz Ziegfeld, he should have known better. One of the myths cultivated by the new industry known as "nostalgia" is that Ziegfeld was a Jew (when I raised the topic with the author of a large tome of Jewish history that had included Ziegfeld in its list of celebrities I was asked incredulously, "Well, wasn't *she* Jewish?"). Another is that Charlie Chaplin was Jewish – a "fact" always denied by Sir Charles himself.

It also goes without saying that people like Bing Crosby, Gene Kelly and Fred Astaire had little problem getting into show business because of their religious faith – although even Astaire has been "claimed" by Jewish publications from time to time. After all, wasn't his name really Austerlitz? It was and so was the place fought over in the Napoleonic wars, and that didn't prove to have much of a Jewish connection either.

Jews have got to the top in the theatre all over the world – but rarely as Jews. They were tops because they were top entertainers. There was, it is true, a great heyday after World War One for what are now known as the "ethnic" comedians, in the United States people like Webber and Fields, Smith and Dale and Fanny Brice – the original "Second-Hand Rose" who never sounded off stage as though she lived surrounded by barrels of pickled herring and mounds of chopped liver, although Barbra Streisand tried to give that impression. There were also the "Yiddisher Mama" songs of Sophie Tucker. In England, in the '30s and '40s there were Jewish dialect comedians like Max Bacon and Issie Bonn. And in both countries, tremendous affection was displayed for a sentimental romp into inter-faith relations called "Abie's Irish Rose".

It is also true that the longest noses in show business

2

belonged to gentiles – W.C. Fields, "Schnozzle" Durante, Danny Thomas and Bob Hope. So caricatures don't prove everything.

Also, it cannot be denied that many of the Jews who went into that multi-coloured, over-amplified world known as show business did so in spite of their background rather than because of it. I can't think of any who used the tremendous power that the stage gave them in order to foster their religious or their political beliefs, although their breasts swelled with charitable intentions – millions of dollars and pounds were raised for Jewish causes by benefit performances. But they raised just as much for Christian and non-sectarian charities.

Compare the number of synagogue scenes in Hollywood films with those set in churches. The fact that Louis B. Mayer insisted on chicken soup being served in the commissary at MGM didn't prevent all his big stars being gentiles.

It is true that Jewish entertainers set up their own social club in Beverly Hills, the Hillcrest – where surrounded by boxes of matzo and menus of traditional, but never kosher, Jewish fare, the old timers who once seemed to dominate much of the Hollywood scene chew the *treifa* fat, discuss the past and prophesy the future. At one time, the club's round table would echo to the sound of Jolson, Burns, Benny, Cantor and Groucho Marx all competing with each other. Groucho Marx, who once said of another establishment that he wouldn't belong to any club that would allow him in as a member. "Now", George Burns told me, "I'm the only one left at the table."

But he has been joined by some other great performers – among them just a few non-Jews, the most celebrated of whom is Jack Lemmon.

Hillcrest was set up largely as a result of the other clubs in the area being what is politely called "restricted". (The Los Angeles Country Club is more than that – not only will it not allow in Jews, it won't grant membership to anyone at all in show business.) But the Jews had their revenge. They struck oil near their golf links!

The Beginning

In the days of what are now fondly remembered as the *shtetls* —
the tiny hamlets in Russia and Poland immortalised in *Fiddler
On The Roof* — the Jew was comforted by two essential
factors: his religion and his family. He never went to the
theatre, never attended a concert, and the idea of the opera
was something that seemed as evil as it was foreign.

Occasionally, however, well-travelled Jews visiting the
shtetls in the area of Russia known as the Pale of Settlement —
usually in order to buy cheaply a product of local workman-
ship or to marry the prettiest girl in town — would tell tales
about the splendours of the ballet or the glories of a performance of *Boris Godunov*. But to the shtetl dweller this knowledge always came second hand and the effect it had on his
imagination was severely limited.

For him, the centre of all life was the synagogue and the
centre of the synagogue was not necessarily the learned rabbi
(who would decide whether a boy or girl could marry or if
freshly-killed chicken had passed the dietary laws and could
be eaten), but the cantor. He it was who could set one shtetl
apart from all the others.

It was the cantor who could keep the men of the village
sitting in stunned quiet for a Saturday morning Sabbath
service that began at 8 o'clock in the morning and could last
until 3 o'clock in the afternoon.

If he were conscientious, he would not only sing the tunes
handed down from generation to generation, but would com-
pose his own repertoire and constantly improvise. If he were
good he would go from village to village, town to town,
spellbinding the worshippers.

The synagogue was house of prayer, house of business and,
although neither the congregations nor the cantors liked to
admit it, also the concert hall.

There were sad, wailing songs for most of the prayers —
there was a great deal to weep for in those days when Czar

Alexander seemed to kill Jews as other monarchs hunted deer and shot birds. But there were also gay, rhythmic melodies usually sung on the festivals and on those joyous family occasions such as weddings and when eight-day-old baby boys who had just been circumcised were welcomed into the fold.

These songs and the style of singing were frequently influenced by the Orthodox Church and, some say, by the very opera platform that from all accounts had seemed so sinful.

But above all they were brought into the home. Children with pure soprano voices were encouraged to join their synagogue choirs. Almost everyone else made an endeavour to sing at the Sabbath meal table and on that most family of all family occasions, the Passover – when on the first night of the festival, fathers told sons and daughters the story of the exodus of the Children of Israel from Egypt.

It was the core around which everything else seemed to be built and to grow.

The music gave the Jew an instinctive, although for generations unrealised, love of the theatre. Just occasionally, however, he did branch out. Dramatic performances of sorts are mentioned in the Talmud and some see "The Song of Songs" penned by King Solomon as being the root of it all. These earliest Jewish plays were the satirical shows put on at the festival of Purim, and based on the story of Queen Esther. These became known as Purim *schpeils*, but they were never seen outside the confines of the Jewish community.

The first time Jews actually played to gentiles was in medieval Italy when the Corso Degli Ebrei – the race of Hebrews – entertained at carnivals.

Then in the nineteenth century, a change became perceptible. Bands of strolling players would come to most of the East European towns, visiting the synagogues first of all. They performed comedies, dramas and, most popular of all, plays that would have the ladies up in the gallery saturating handkerchieves with their tears. Always the plays would be in their own vernacular – Yiddish. Very often the stories would be about communities like their own, set in synagogues like theirs and about people like themselves.

Music and Theatre

The musical accompaniment would be provided by the local violinist – the fiddler who, contrary to the now prevalent image, usually had his feet on the ground, even if his head was often in the clouds, if not on the roof.

The fiddler – and in the bigger communities there grew up string ensembles to play on big local occasions, particularly at outdoor wedding ceremonies and receptions – became one of the principal local characters. The violin was the instrument that Jewish mothers wanted their sons to play as much as in later generations they wanted them to become doctors and lawyers.

In short, the violin became *the* Jewish instrument – and the players the ancestors of the world's greatest violinists. As someone once said: "It's easy to see why. Can you imagine *schlepping* a grand piano with you from one pogrom to the next?".

There is more truth in that than might at first meet the eye. Few will deny the pre-eminence of the Jewish violinist: Yehudi Menuhin, Isaac Stern, Jasha Heifetz, the Oistrackhs, Nathan Milstein ... the list goes on and on. But it was the instrument of exile. Today, Israelis mourn the dearth of new violinists – with the obvious exceptions of Pinchas Zuckerman and Itzhak Perlman – and marvel at the unprecedented number of pianists being turned out in the country.

It was through music that the twin bulwarks of Jewish life, the family and the synagogue, came together. And they gave birth to the Yiddish theatre. This is generally accepted as having been founded in 1876 in Romania, in the capital of the Moldavian province, Jasi. There, in that year, Abraham Goldfaden produced his first play *The Green Tree Inn*.

When in the nineteenth century the first Jews left Eastern

6

Europe for the United States and, to a much smaller extent, Britain, they took with them, as well as a love for their home and their religion, that devotion to music and a subliminal attachment to the stage.

To America

The early immigrants looked back on their ghetto music with yearning. They established in exile their Yiddish theatre to an extent that had been practically unknown in the ghetto. To the stage they brought not just their experience of persecution and their escape but also their memories of the fiery preachers who, like the itinerant cantor, went from town to town warning of the dangers of evil living and the joys unknown of the coming of a Messianic age.

In the dirty, lice-ridden sweatshops and the filthy tenements from which there seemed no immediate prospect of escape, the imaginations of the young immigrants ran riot. The young people combined a perhaps natural quality of exhibitionism with a thorough determination to pull themselves up by their bootstraps and escape from their environment.

Even if the streets of New York were not paved with gold, their expectation was as gilded as were their memories of the past. Some of them went out to sell ribbons from barrows and pushcarts in the streets of the Lower East Side and the alleys and lanes of London's East End. Others had nothing to sell but themselves. But sell they did.

From the pushcarts came commercial empires and from the courtyards of the tenements and the platforms of the settlement houses came the men and women who were about to revolutionise the theatre.

In America, one generation alone produced not only a cluster of stars who had customers drooling for a dime-a-time in the same way that Caruso wowed the well-heeled patrons at the Met, but also the people who helped create the legend that the show must go on – the men who put the business into show business.

The Impresarios

The Shubert brothers discovered a young entertainer called Al Jolson and gave Ziegfeld a run for his money. Sam Harris teamed up with Cohan and then with a prolific song writer called Irving Berlin to establish the Music Box Theatre and with it, the Music Box Revue. George White produced the famous Scandals; Rufus Le Maire, the Affairs; Earl Carrol, the Vanities; and Billy Rose would write songs, produce shows and marry Fanny Brice.

There was also Gus Edwards, one of the most enterprising of all theatrical impresarios, and before him David Belasco and the Frohmann Brothers, one of whom was drowned when the liner Lusitania sank. (They had a niece, Jane Froman, who became a singing star of the late '30s and early '40s and whose life story was told in the film *With A Song In My Heart*.)

Meanwhile, a man called Minsky was finding out the hard way just how far a girl with shapely breasts and thighs could go in baring her body on a public stage. When he was sure, an entirely new, strictly American, convention was truly established – burlesque, or the "old burleycue" as the professionals liked to call it.

While Minsky toiled, two rather unpleasant gentlemen by the names of Abe Erlanger and Mark Klaw tried to carve up the whole of vaudeville between them, with an organisation – eventually outlawed – known by the sinister name of the Syndicate.

On the other side of the business, a certain William Morris – once the proprietor of a chain (or circuit) of vaudeville theatres – had established, next to another Jewish-controlled conglomerate, MCA, the biggest ten per-center of all time, the William Morris Agency.

At the same settlement houses where performers were honing their acts, a young immigrant called Sol Hurok was cutting his own teeth – readying himself for the day when he would bring Chaliapin, Galli-Curci and Pavlova to America.

He became the greatest impresario of the New York ballet, opera house and concert hall.

The opera would have to wait at least two generations before it provided any Jewish *performers* of note, but eventually Richard Tucker, Robert Merrill, Jan Peerce and Beverly Sills would become stars of the Met and Miss Sills its director.

The American story was repeated to some degree throughout the world.

Soviet Union

The story of Jews in the Russian theatre is indicative of the general position of Jews in the country as a whole. During the years of the ghettos, they were where they were expected to be. When the ghetto walls were pulled down and Jews moved out of the shtetl and the Pale of Settlement, so they entered the Russian theatre. They became actors on stage, dancers in the ballet, stars on screen, clowns in the circus – some of the finest clowns were Jews. Then when it became less fashionable to be Jewish and Jews were purged from other walks of life, so their presence in the performing arts was, shall we say, "discouraged". The Jews who remained did not always like their origins to be known.

But there they certainly were – men like Serge Eisenstein, one of the world's greatest film directors.

The East European film industry has had a vast injection of Jewish talent, although it may be loath to recognise it as such. Nevertheless, the Czechs Milos Forman and Hugo Haas are giants in their field. So is the Hungarian Jan Kadar.

From Russia in the 1970s came, too, the celebrated dissidents Valery and Galena Panov, who helped Israel to establish its first important link with ballet.

Israel

Israel's own theatre has its roots in the Yiddish stage, but even in post-Revolutionary Russia the Habima was performing in

9

Hebrew. It settled in Palestine during the days of the British mandate — theatrical performances had been introduced to that country in the 1880s — with tours of small theatrical troupes going from settlement to settlement.

If a country is mirrored by its theatre, then Israel as a melting pot of the nations has for long had a fairly representative stage. In many ways, that has been its problem. Its actors and directors were presenting English plays in English, German plays in German and Russian plays in Russian while Israel was still searching for her true identity. Too often the national thirst for culture was only partly satisfied — by Hebrew translations of foreign plays that don't always translate too well.

The problem was accentuated by a deep embarrassment on the part of the modern Israeli theatre companies and their audiences concerning their history. When they did look for a theatre that was their own, they found themselves uncomfortable with the past, now symbolised again by the Yiddish theatre.

The young *sabras* hated the language of exile and didn't want it to be thought that those awkward, pale-faced, pathetic creatures in Yiddish literature were their own ancestors. They had not yet come to terms with the holocaust — which to some was a matter of national disgrace as much as of national tragedy. They hated the Yiddish theatre even more — even though none of them would deny that it *was* the first genuine Jewish drama movement. They saw themselves as part of a bright new country full of new strengths, new ideals. It was a view that changed dramatically after the 1967 Six-Day War when they recognised the brotherhood of world Jewry. The theatre changed, too.

Quite suddenly, the groundwork laid by the Habima and other pioneering theatrical ventures is paying off. An Israeli theatre with an Israeli identity finally looks as though it is blooming into maturity. In its way, even more important, it is producing artists of international renown who work in the country and represent it abroad. Chaim Topol is perhaps its

10

number one public relations status symbol. But one should not forget either the winners of the Eurovision Song Contest in two successive years – Avi Cohen with "Aba-Nibi" in 1978, Israel's thirtieth anniversary year, and Milk and Honey with "Hallelujah" the day before Israel signed its peace treaty with Egypt.

France

France produced one of the most legendary actresses of all time – Sarah Bernhardt, the "Divine Sarah" who was one of the great personalities of the Comédie Française, and who in old age and with one leg amputated played England's Queen Elizabeth in what was perhaps the first historical feature film.

She was born in 1844 of a Jewish father and a Catholic mother, and was baptised as a child, but she always spoke of her Jewish roots with pride.

More recently Sacha Distel has brightened France's pop scene. Yves Montand and his wife Simone Signoret have shone in the film world, as too does Anouk Aimée, a glamour figure of the post-war years. Directors have included Claude Lelouch, Claude Berry and, perhaps one of the most important names of the cinema of the 1970s, the Polish-born Roman Polanski.

Abel Gance, whose work is only now being appreciated internationally as a result of the recent rediscovery of his magnificent *Napoleon* epic, has for long been accepted in his native land as one of its most outstanding directors.

And one of France's greatest comedy actors – indeed he was for years known as the French Chaplin – was Max Linder, who, unfettered by spoken dialogue, had audiences all over the world falling out of their seats.

Germany

At one time, there were said to be 2,400 Jewish actors and theatrical directors in Germany. Hitler put a stop to that, and a theatre that could boast one of the most brilliant directors of all time, Max Reinhardt, found itself with a tremendous void when he and the other Jews had gone. Germany lost Reinhardt to Hollywood where he made a strange version of *A Midsummer Night's Dream*, starring Mickey Rooney, James Cagney and Joe E. Brown.

The influence of German immigrants on Hollywood is justly legendary. Josef von Sternberg – at one time seen as the Svengali to Marlene Dietrich's *Trilby* – came over at much the same time as Erich von Stroheim (how the Nazis must have hated the idea of a Jew portraying the typical German *Junker* aristocrat). Like "Von", Otto Preminger doubled as an actor and director. William Wyler, Billy Wilder and Fred Zimmerman all came along the same Teutonic route before settling among the California palms.

The German film industry also boasted – until Hitler that is – Anton Walbrook and Elizabeth Bergner among its number. Their loss was Britain's gain.

They were not the only ones. Louise Rainer joined Peter Lorre and Max Ophuls (in his case, via Paris) in the United States. At much the same time, Kurt Weill, whose *Threepenny Opera* made a lasting mark, left for America too. If he never achieved so much again, his *Lady In The Dark* was a brilliant try.

Denmark

Even Denmark – that most tolerant of European nations – was to lose a major theatrical personality to Hollywood because of the Nazi occupation. Victor Borge, the pianist-humorist who invented his own form of musical punctuation and was to tell his own one-sided view of the life of the composers, settled in the United States and became an international star. An achievement he could never have imagined when studying in an ultra-Orthodox Hebrew school in Copenhagen before his barmitzvah, as Borge Rosenbaum.

Great Britain

Britain's Jewish theatrical connections date back further than those in most other countries. As long ago as 1800, some claim that Edmund Kean, a great character actor in the style of Henry Irving, was a Jew.

Jews were active in other parts of the theatrical world too. One of the earliest Jewish actresses in England was Hannah Norsa, daughter of an Italian Jew and who in 1732 had been in the original cast of *The Beggars Opera*. She played Polly Peachum.

For years, Jews acted in the great dramas — and sang in the music halls. In the smoke-laden, beer-drenched atmosphere of these establishments, men and women — the men in cloth caps, the women in large feathered hats that owed little to good taste and sometimes a great deal to the milliners — joined in the choruses of the "Tar-ra-ra-boom-de-ay" girl. Among these was Lottie Collins and her equally famous daughter Josie; their film star descendant Joan had a similar effect on cinema and TV audiences in the 1960s, '70s and '80s. Coming from a similar background, Ethel Leavey went to America, married George M. Cohan and became a vaudeville and Broadway favourite.

In Britain, too, Chaim Reuven Weintrop became Bud Flanagan, one of the best-loved artists ever to appear on a British stage. Later on still, Frank Ableson became Frankie Vaughan, at about the same time as a girl with a tickly voice called Alma Cogan was a top attraction. Helen Shapiro didn't change her name, just her gymslip and became a teenage pop idol of the early '60s.

On screen, there were international stars like Claire Bloom and Yvonne Mitchell and Janet Suzman, who was also a bulwark of the National Theatre. Hermione Gingold tantalised Maurice Chevalier in *Gigi*. Ada Reeve was one of the original Gaiety Girls. The music hall was replete with Jewish names, ranging from the 25-stone Teddy Brown to Nat Mills

13

and Bobbie who later became radio stars.

Marty Feldman, whom I personally remember as being a show off as well as a showman when we were both pupils at Luton Grammar School and attended the local Hebrew classes, in a very short time graduated from British TV comedy writing and performing to become a top star in American films – most notably in Mel Brook's *Silent Movie*. He died in 1982.

In the span of a few years, director John Schlesinger, actors Herbert Lom and Sidney James – originally from South Africa but regarded as the archetype film cockney – all made their mark.

This is essentially a study of entertainers, but one factor must be stressed – the tremendous contribution of the Jewish playwrights of the '60s, a subject for a book of its own. Suffice to say that without names like Harold Pinter, Arnold Wesker and Bernard Kops the English-language theatre would be a very different and much poorer place.

The constantly changing world of popular music was given an enormous jolt when a very young British businessman named Brian Epstein discovered a group of boys who he thought would do rather better if they were known as the Beatles.

A couple of years before that, a song writer called Lionel Bart wrote a hit show called *Oliver*, eventually to become a highly successful film musical and provide the cinema with one of its most exciting – although insufficiently used – talents, Ron Moody.

The most successful personality of them all was undoubtedly Peter Sellers, descendant of the famous Jewish boxer Daniel Mendoza, who leapt from comedian in the BBC Radio Goon Show to international fame as an actor, suitor of Liza Minnelli and superstar in the "Pink Panther" series.

They were all carrying on a tradition of British film making launched by names like Sir Alexander Korda and Sir Michael Balcon.

Robert Rietty, son of the Italian Jewish actor Victor Rietti,

14

was also a prominent actor in British films and now runs probably the world's most successful film dubbing business in the world. He has done a great deal to popularise Israeli films in Britain.

For the past 20 years, there have been notable performances from David Kossoff, who told Bible stories, an unusual career for a man who had once seemed the stereotyped Jewish tailor. Alfie Bass and Alfred Marks also had their place in British theatre. In film and TV comedy roles there was Bernard Breslau. In TV alone, Mike and Bernie Winters. In the circus, Coco the clown.

But the real dictators of British entertainment since the war have been the Winowgradsky family – or, as they are better known, Lord Grade and Lord Delfont. With his brother Bernard Delfont, Lew Grade was a Charleston dancer – not very good ones, according to their sister Rita. With his brother Leslie, he was a leading agent. Lew and Bernard were knighted and made peers of the realm – and Lew smoked the biggest cigars since the ones used by Winston Churchill. For years, he and Bernard between them virtually were the British film industry – until even they couldn't resist the power of an international take-over bid.

In their day, the Winowgradsky family enjoyed the Yiddish theatre which flourished almost as successfully as that in New York. Morris Moscovitch would appear at the theatres in the Mile End Road, from which, occasionally, an actor would be discovered and make his mark on the West End stage or the screen. Meir Tzelniker was one – although he was forever cast as the contract Jew.

United States

But it was in the United States that the Yiddish theatre made its almost unbelievable impact.

For the immigrant in New York, the Yiddish theatre was more than just a diversion from the sweat shop, a solace from

15

the worries of disease and poverty, and a link with the so recent past. It was also a means of watching the incredibly powerful giants of the stage who in the old British actor-manager tradition combined Jewish business acumen with the right dose of schmaltz – perhaps a preferable word in this connection to "ham".

Mothers would bring their children and keep them fed with a constant supply of pickled herring and bagels throughout the performance. If the actors were not up to scratch the herring tails would be thrown on to the stage. But if they were good, the people out front would serenade the company with a chorus of "ahs" when everything was nice and cosy and "oy-oy-oy" when, very much more frequently, things were not.

The German Jews who had arrived in New York ahead of the swarm of Russian and Polish immigrants did not like the Yiddish actors at all. They, like their language, seemed to represent the ghetto from which these 'aristocrats' of the city had always held themselves aloof.

Within five years of their arrival some of the young people in the immigrant families – the *fineshmeckers* (nice smellers) of Second Avenue as the players called them – considered they knew much more about the theatre than the common Yiddish players, and tried to tell their parents and friends how unfashionable they all were. But the Yiddish theatre was more powerful than they and always seemed to win. Indeed, it would survive for another 50 years.

On the Lower East Side in halls a stone's throw from the pushcarts of Delancey and Orchard Streets and on Second Avenue they could marvel at Moscovitch (who found greater success than he had achieved in London), weep with Boris Tomashefsky and wonder at the sheer talent of Jacob Adler, his wife Sarah and their children, Celia, Frances, Julia, Stella and Luther.

Luther Adler became an outstanding film actor. Nor was he the only product of the Yiddish stage to do so. Emmanuel Goldenberg became Edward G. Robinson and Muni Weisenfreund, the most illustrious star of the gangster era, Paul

16

Muni, the "Scarface" who also was Zola, Pasteur and Juarez.

More important than the effect that the Yiddish theatre had on its audiences was the traumatic experience it represented for its performers. In the ghettos, the Yiddish actor had been – like the shoemaker, the tailor, the coachman or the milkman – an artisan. He was no more worldly-wise than they were; as much influenced by the synagogue or the urge for revolution as anyone else. The universe then was no bigger than the distance that could be travelled for a couple of roubles.

Then suddenly, in what had become the biggest Jewish city in the world, they discovered they could, at the drop of a hat (and for the first time many of them really were dropping their hats, that most evident of all symbols of Orthodoxy) see gentiles walking in the streets, and even talk to them. Before long, they were marrying them, too. Much more important, the Yiddish theatres, just as the choir lofts of the synagogues, became haunts of the impresarios and talent scouts.

It was a gateway to freedom and independence. The Yiddish theatres even opened on Friday nights and Saturdays – such desecrations as would not have been considered in *der heim*.

Stock characters like the snuff-sniffing synagogue beadle (the *shammas*) and the umbrella-carrying marriage broker, (the *shadchan*) abounded. The customers loved plays like *Yankel Boila*, *Der Pogrom* and S.An-Ski's *Dybbuk*. But they also rejoiced in marvelling at the picturesque verses of a Yiddish King Lear – "Ah, such vonderful tings you can say in *mamaloshen*" – by Jacob Adler and William Shakespeare.

To some that environment gave its performers justly-deserved fame. Others were not quite so lucky. David Opatoshu, a young actor of the Yiddish theatre – and of its weak and short-lived offspring the New York-based Yiddish cinema – deserved to make a bigger impact than he did in the few films and TV plays that have come his way. Only in *Exodus* did he have a chance to really shine.

Muni and Robinson were part of that group which can be collectively described as "The Incredible Generation". As for the others, they were – the Marx Brothers, the Ritz Brothers,

George Jessel and Harry Richman, Fanny Brice and Sophie Tucker, Jack Benny and his great friend George Burns, Eddie Cantor and the king of them all Al Jolson.

Quite clearly, they were not the first Jewish show-biz stars — and remember that 70 years ago, hearts beat fast and strong for a young woman born Thedosia Goodman, but whom audiences knew better as Theda Bara, a sultry temptress if ever there was one — but never before had there been a group of actors and other entertainers who together made such an impact — and I doubt there will ever be one again.

They were either immigrants or children of immigrants who had just begun to make it big and they all did it, give or take a few years, at the same time. You have only got to see the rosta at meetings of the Friars Club to realise how important they were.

Together they formed a group as daunting as any rat pack that would later surround Humphrey Bogart or Frank Sinatra. Photographs of them sitting at table still adorn Broadway restaurants — and well they might. They may not have adhered strictly to the Jewish dietary laws, but the delights of kosher corned beef, matzo ball soup and sour pickled cucumbers could not be lightly left behind. At one time there was a whole industry supplying these delicacies to the Broadway dressing rooms.

They made their real impact on the stage and later in the studios of Hollywood. For the whole of the 1930s and, it could be argued, until the 1950s — they were the nucleus on which American entertainment was built.

A freemasonry developed around them. In private, they were consumed by jealousy and there was nothing as galling or as effective as a rival's adoring notice or a set of impressive box office figures to encourage the others to do even better. But in public, they kissed and hugged each other at every visible opportunity.

At the Friars Club, they insulted each other one moment, played poker the next and then lauded their brothers at a whole succession of evenings devoted to the greatest god of them all, Success. If one of them was in trouble, the others would fly east-to-west to do a good turn – especially if there were cameramen and radio microphones around to record the event.

If in life they quarrelled, in death they were spiritual blood brothers. The men who put on the biggest, best, most super, colossal shows in the theatre and in Hollywood could stage a funeral that matched any theatrical spectacle. There was no appearance that could compete with the majesty of acting as a pallbearer. George Jessel, the original "Jazz Singer", made a virtual profession of funeral eulogies. Not for nothing was he known as America's Toastmaster General.

Having said that, there is also no doubt that friendships could be true and lasting. The tears that welled in the eyes of George Burns at the funeral of Jack Benny were real, and the lump in his throat choking his words as he struggled to form an eulogy could not have been more genuine.

They were the most charitable group of individuals who ever assembled under one roof. In the 1930s, they set up the Jewish Theatrical League – as a rival to the Catholic Actors' Guild, but also to do good, both publicly and privately.

It was established originally as the Jewish Theatrical Guild of America Inc., with William Morris as its President, Eddie Cantor first Vice President, Sam Bernard (prominent vaude-villian and Ziegfeld comedian) second Vice President and Sime Silverman, founder Editor of *Variety*, third Vice President.

The members were promised "interment of deceased in need; annual impressive and sacred memorial services in memory of our departed members".

It would be "the first time in history that Judaism is per-petuated in the theatrical profession".

The introductory leaflet emphasised that it would, above all, "contribute to charity". Its dues were $10 annually or a life membership of $250. Prospective members tried to work out the cheaper rate before deciding which membership to take.

Together, they set up the Actors' Temple, Ezrath Israel at 339 West 47th Street – an Orthodox Synagogue, whose spiritual leader Rabbi Bernstein was as talented a "turn" as any who trod the boards of the Palace.

His best performance would be on Yom Kippur, the Day of Atonement, when even show-biz moguls who were most happy looking over a balance sheet would turn their eyes to a prayer book. That was the day Rabbi Bernstein would have his appeal for funds for the synagogue or some other charity.

The diminutive Rabbi would give "billing" to his cast sitting both in the stalls – the downstairs pews – and in the gallery (since it was an Orthodox establishment, that was where the ladies were sent, no matter how important they were).

"Eddie Cantor," he would begin, "starring in *Kid Boots* at the Ziegfeld Theatre, how much? $1,000 – $2,000?

"George Jessel at the Winter Garden, $500 – $1,000?" Whatever he was offered, he doubled the sum from the pulpit – and the money always came in. When Sophie Tucker made her donation from the balcony, the performance was better than ever. She offered $1,000.

But the rabbi's pitch was predictable: "Sophie Tucker ... our darling Sophella, God bless you. Where are you appearing, darling? Oh ... Sophie Tucker, now playing at the Riverside Theatre – that's on 96th Street, ain't it? ... $2,000!"

Ask the rabbi about attendance at Yiskor – the memorial prayers recited on Yom Kippur and the last days of festivals – and Dr Bernstein would point out that he had such big attendances he had to hold the services in two stages. "The first show wasn't so good, but it was SRO (standing room only) for the second performance," he reported to delighted members of his congregation.

Today actors like Walter Matthau and Buddy Hackett can be seen even more frequently in Hollywood taking an active part in services of the Temple of the Performing Arts whose

20

congregation is made almost exclusively of people from the film industry.

But the heyday of the Jewish entertainer was in Rabbi Bernstein's day – the 1930s – the decade of The Incredible Generation.

Anti-Semitism?

Just occasionally, however, the Jewish influence did seem to sow the seed of anti-Semitism.

And if, as Al Jolson said, the theatre was tolerant in America and anti-Semitism was strictly frowned upon in vaudeville – you couldn't make jokes about Jews on the American stage and get away with them – it was not quite the same in England.

In 1930, a London paper lamented: "Every Yom Kippur embarrasses scores of stage artists, for more of our leading performers are Jews than we remember. When the music hall was a popular institution, dozens of deputies had to be found suddenly, so numerous were the Jewish absentees."

Indeed, there is a story about an actor called Carl Hertz who was ordered to perform at a music hall on the Day of Atonement. "If you insist, I will do so," he said. "But you must put it in writing. Then, I can read the letter from the stage." He was allowed the day off.

Sophie Tucker used to compromise. She wouldn't eat anything from dusk on the day before Yom Kippur until the evening of the fast itself. A heavy smoker, she wouldn't light a single cigarette – but she performed just the same.

The late Hannen Swaffer, never considered an anti-Semite, wrote in the *Daily Express* in 1929: " I wonder why Jews are still so clannish about artists of their own race. They are no longer a subject people, herded together in ghettos or in the back streets of great cities.

"When they were, you could understand their delight at the prominence achieved by one of their number. Today they rank equally with the other citizens of most of the countries in which they live. Yet, sometimes I find in theatres they become almost annoying because of the way in which they applaud a co-religionist."

He could not understand why bandleader Abe Lyman had scored such a hit at the London Palladium – "the moment his number was announced it seems hundreds of Jews who were scattered all over the house began to applaud with a rapture usually only heard by artists who have returned to their country after long absences."

And he went on: "I notice this myself often at a theatre. I have seen Anita Elson applauded more loudly by Jewish people in the audience than by the gentiles."

He could not understand how an actress got louder applause than anyone else. "Oh, she belongs to the family," said a friend. He meant she was Jewish. One tends to doubt whether Swaffer's "friend" ever existed.

Even *Variety*, the show-biz Bible as it is popularly known – one could almost call it the show-biz Torah – was not immune to contemplating this Jewish influence. The paper was founded by Sime Silverman; all its editors have been Jews. Yet in December 1920 they could ponder the question of "A Syncopated Symphony":

"There is one vocation, all the known members of which could pass a synagogue door unchallenged," it reported.

"No? Look at the list: Al Jolson, Ted Lewis, Sophie Tucker, Nora Bayes, Willie Howard, Eddie Cantor, Fanny Brice, Nora Helperin, Georgie Price, Gus Edwards, Lillian Shaw, Belle Baker, Ruth Royes, Rai Samuels, Flo Adler, Anna Chandler – everyone of them a syncopate and every one of them a Jew.

"There is something about that kind of metre that seems to come naturally with the heritage of the race. Its own music, the unwritten classics chanted by the holy cantors preserved them through the generations since David strummed his harp; but while today there still lingers in every kosher soul [!] a passionate love of the Judaic hymns, those words of Israel's heartbreak, those moons of exile and despair, there rips from the lips of the same children of God's chosen, the most intoxicating and saleable rags, jazz and blues."

There was a time when American vaudevillians were advised to drop – of all things – the name Arthur because it looked too Jewish. Certainly, many did change their names. Eddie Cantor was originally Isidor Iskowich. Al Jolson was Asa Yoelson. Lee J. Cobb was born Leo Jacob.

New Generations

The period of Jewish influence did not die with World War Two. After the Jolson generation came performers like Danny Kaye – so unique an entertainer that he deserves not to be linked to any group at all – Phil Silvers, Milton Berle, Mel Torme and Dinah Shore, among a host of others.

It is perhaps because of the cantorial tradition that American show business has rarely been without its top Jewish singers. There was, for instance, the sensation of the 1950s and '60s – and not simply because he married Elizabeth Taylor – Eddie Fisher, a protégé of Eddie Cantor and devoted admirer of Al Jolson. Bob Dylan, a sometime convert to Christianity, had an amazing impact on the folk music scene.

Simon and Garfunkel, Neil Diamond and Barry Manilow have become well known in the American entertainment scene – with Diamond's own lyrical vocalising style making him a not unreasonable choice for a new stab at the Jolson role in the 1981 remake of *The Jazz Singer*.

But his greatest success has come from records and concert audiences of a size of which Jolson could only dream – although *he* experienced the unbounded adoration of Broadway, as well as the theatres up and down the States that he made his own.

Barry Manilow's experience has been much the same as Diamond's although he hasn't to date made any feature films. He has, however, been responsible – if reports to the effect are accurate – for a whole string of broken marriages throughout

the world. There is something in the Manilow make-up —
blond hair, large nose — that makes women whom he has never
met want to leave their husbands, or at least travel thousands
of miles to see him. Along with many others, he has found it
advantageous to cash in on his Jewish background — a recent
book made much play of photographs taken on the day of his
barmitzvah — but unlike some others, he has frequently been a
large-scale donor to Jewish causes, and shows a distinct pride
in Israel.

Similarly, Steve Lawrence and Eydie Gorme have gone on
record, talking a great deal about their 1983 visit to Israel —
with Eydie adding details of the kosher recipes she learned
from her Turkish-Jewish grandmother. Undoubtedly, Jewish
audiences wanted to hear exactly that.

Jewish comedians Mort Sahl, Lenny Bruce and Woody
Allen fitted perfectly into the tradition set by their forebears of
The Generation. One of the most original entertainers of the
'60s and '70s — coming to international attention with the film
Cabaret — started life as one of the Mickey Katz Kittens and
later changed his name to Joel Grey. The most successful?
Take your pick from Dustin Hoffman and Barbra Streisand.

The Song Writers

Great as the contribution of Jewish performers and producers
has been, that of the songwriters and the men who invented
the modern musical — Richard Rodgers and Oscar Hammerstein II, and three of the Big Four, George Gershwin (and
brother Ira), Irving Berlin and Jerome Kern — was equally
outstanding. Only Cole Porter stands out as a Wasp, a White
Anglo-Saxon Protestant. He once told Sammy Cahn, another
important contributor to the Jewish show-biz story, that if he,
like Cahn, had been born on the East Side, he could have
become a genius.

Cahn — who began his music career by playing Yiddish
songs on the piano for his mother — teamed up with other

Jewish songwriters like Saul Chaplin and Julie Styne.

In a previous age, there had been Sigmund Romberg and Rudolf Friml. Richard Rodgers' first partner was Lorenz Hart. Long before Rodgers and Hart wrote the score of *Pal Joey*, Arthur Schwartz and Howard Dietz were putting together a revue for Fred Astaire and his sister Adele, called *The Bandwagon*.

Later, another synagogue cantor's son, Harold Arlen, writer of "That Old Black Magic", "Stormy Weather" and "I've Got the World on a String" joined with E.Y. Harburg to provide Judy Garland with her most famous number "Over The Rainbow".

Among the great post-war musical hits were a whole succession of shows from *Finian's Rainbow* to *My Fair Lady* and *Camelot* by Frederic Loewe and Alan J. Lerner.

Frank Loesser wrote *Guys and Dolls*. Richard Adler and Jerry Ross produced *Damn Yankees* and *The Pajama Game*.

The musical genius Leonard Bernstein lent his talents to the Broadway stage first for *On the Town* and *Wonderful Town*, then for *West Side Story*. He was not prevented, however, from also writing a new score for the Mass.

The most Jewish show of all was to come from Sheldon Harnick and Jerry Bock. *Fiddler On The Roof* proved to be the biggest success of his career for Jewish actor/comedian Zero Mostel in America, and on the London stage and later on the screen for the Israeli, Chaim Topol. Later, Harnick and Bock would just fail to repeat that magic with a show about the Jewish family of financial princes, the Rothschilds.

Jerry Herman tried an Israeli theme with the musical *Milk and Honey* but did much better with *Hello Dolly* and *Mame*.

Marvin Hamlisch, creator of *A Chorus Line*, is undoubtedly heir to the Rodgers and Hammerstein–Lerner and Loewe tradition, with a score of tunes that could justify his quoting himself a dozen times a day. After all, he did write *They're Playing My Song*. Although still young, he has proved he has staying power – perhaps rather more than Burt Bacharach and Hal David, the blue-eyed boys of popular music in the '60s and

25

early '70s, who haven't done a great deal in recent years.

What worked on the Broadway stage did not always do quite so well on the screen – even in the days when musical films were as essential an ingredient of people's cinema diets as a bag of popcorn. One important reason was that the film was international. Broadway theatre could not live without its Jewish patrons, who filled up most of the seats and often provided as much entertainment with their conversations shouted from one seat to another as did the show on stage.

I can remember a round of applause for a "Becky" who told "Sadie" four rows behind her how she had managed to get a pair of "twofors" – two tickets for the price of one.

Years before *Fiddler* and *Mame*, Moss Hart was writing and directing Broadway hits. Long after him, the top American impresarios would be David Merrick and Alexander H. Cohen.

Television in America could boast among its stars Lorne Greene, Efrem Zimbalist Junior, Gene Barry and a host of lesser names.

Of the most successful theatrical writing teams few could compare with Betty Comden and Adolph Green, who did *Bells Are Ringing, Wonderful Town* and *The Band Wagon*.

Theatrical history was not only made by Jews, it was also recorded by them. Columnists Walter Winchell, Bernard Sobel and Sidney Skolsky were as influential as the editor of *Variety*.

It was a non-Jewish American writer who said in the mid-1970s: "The truth of the matter is, the entire cultural press, publishing, criticism, television ... theatre ... is almost 90 per cent Jewish orientated. I mean, I can't count on one hand five people of importance – of real importance – in the media who aren't Jewish. I can't."

It wasn't any more true then than were the doubts expressed about the reality of Jewish domination of Big Business.

And yet ... and yet ...

For every Jewish entertainer there has been another born of WASP parentage. But then compare the number of White

26

Anglo-Saxon Protestant families with Jews in the populations of any country outside Israel and you can begin to understand the dilemma.

Humour

Can you divorce Jewish humour from all this? You can't. But that is another book entirely. Or if you like, another library. Nevertheless, it is through what people regard as Jewish humour that audiences become conscious of the Jewish contribution to entertainment.

Listen to a Jewish story or two and you understand a little more clearly why it was that over the years so many Jews did tread the boards.

"Moshe," called his wife as an air-raid siren sounded in an Israeli border town. "I'm not going into the shelter till I find my teeth."

"Your *teeth*?" he asked despairing for her sanity. "Your teeth? What do you think they're dropping out there? Sandwiches?"

Or the beggar who knocked on the door of the imposing New York brownstone house, hoping for food.

"Would you take yesterday's soup?" asked the buxom prosperous-looking woman.

"Sure," he says, smiling.

"Then come back tomorrow."

Or the Jewish crime boss who is gunned down in a hail of bullets as he knocks on his mother's door.

"Mama, mama," he pleads with the last breath in his blood-drenched body.

"Shush," the old woman commands. "First we eat. Then we talk."

Mothers, food. Two cornerstones on which Jewish comedians made their reputation, their fortunes and established a folk industry. An industry which in its way was as important and ethnically vital as the production of clothes and furniture.

The roots of it all are in Yiddish.

27

So Lets Hear The Applause

What other language could produce words like *dappes* which as Leo Rosten says in his delightful book *The Joys of Yiddish* came straight out of the garment industry?

As he explains, the man who drops an iron is a *schlemeil*. The one on whose foot it falls is a *schlemazel*. *Dappes* is the man standing at the back saying "tsk, tsk, tsk ..." in sounds as musical as any of the songs performed on the Yiddish stage.

It was an essentially immigrant humour, as translatable from one ghetto to another as herrings and beigels and perpetuated for new generations who knew neither sweatshops nor even potato lutkas or chopped liver, by such as Neil Simon and Mel Brooks.

The Bands

And before we go into specifics, let us pause ever so briefly to talk about those other musical sounds – the ones performed by the Jewish bandleaders. In Britain, names such as Stanley Black, Joe Loss, Geraldo, Ambrose, Harry Gold and Nat Temple; in America, a sweep of names: Artie Shaw, Benny Goodman, Sammy Kaye, Ted Lewis, Ziggy Elman, Ben Bernie, Abe Lyman, Gux Arnhem and that genius of the drums, Ben Pollack.

To this list, mind you, Joe Loss will add a score of non-Jewish names who were just as influential, if not more so – Glenn Miller, the Dorseys, Henry Mancini in America; Jack Hylton, Jack Payne and Henry Hall in Britain. As Loss says:

"The Jewish boys mostly came from the East End, the sons of tailors and cabinet makers. All were given violins or some other musical instrument as kids in an effort to improve themselves. Some took to it. Some didn't."

Those who did were spared becoming tailors and cabinet makers. Those who didn't became ... doctors, lawyers, big businessmen – and tailors and cabinet makers.

What Loss did not agree with was that little aspect of band life which tended to be hushed up – anti-Semitism.

The way some people tell it, the non-Jewish bands positively refused to employ Jewish musicians – even if one or two of them employed a Jewish "fixer" to handle the business side of things.

The Film Industry

For years it seemed that Jews were being kept out of the movies too, but this time *by* Jews. They were not being kept out of the studio business offices, but they rarely became the subject of Hollywood films or starred in them as the glamour figures.

Hollywood is where the streets are paved with Goldwyn and Mayer and Warner. The big Hollywood moguls, as everyone must know, *were* mostly Jews – Louis B. Mayer of MGM, Adolph Zukor of Paramount, Carl Lamelle of Universal, Harry Cohn and his brother Jack of Columbia; the Warner Brothers. Only United Artists and Twentieth Century–Fox, run by the Greek Spyrus P. Skouras and his brilliant production head, the non-Jewish Darryl F. Zanuck were known as the "Goyishe studios".

But they didn't like Jewish stars. For years, the less than handsome East European-born studio bosses sought a kind of beauty for their movies that was not seen on the streets of the shtetl. As if it were a way of cleansing themselves, making them feel more trim, or perhaps more Anglo-Saxon and more All-American, they sought stars who seemed cleaner than clean, whiter than white.

Of course, there were exceptions: Lauren Bacall, John Garfield, Dane Clark, Kirk Douglas, Tony Curtis (born Bernie Schwartz), Judy Holliday, the late Melvin Douglas, Sam Jaffe, Jerry Lewis – born Joseph Levitch – Paul Lukas, Molly Picon, Sylvia Sidney, Shelley Winters, Paulette Goddard, Lily Palmer, Herbert Lom, Peter Lorre, Alan Arkin, Luise Rainer, Ed Wynn and his son Keenan, Zero Mostel – and *Guys and Dolls* would never have been the same without Stubby Kaye "rocking the boat."

And, of course names like Edward G. Robinson and Paul

Muni. But in that paragraph, you have most of them. There are certain publications who would like to "claim" Paul Newman, too. But his mother was not Jewish and that definition would not stand up in a Beth Din.

However, as the cinema changed, so did its ideas of beauty and its feelings about its Jewish performers. How else could Streisand and Hoffman have made it so big? And today, James Caan and George Segal – who in 1983 married in a London synagogue – are big enough in the box office stakes.

Then there is Gene Wilder – who first became a name to notice opposite Zero Mostel in the 1968 success *The Producers* – and Carl Reiner, Mel Brooks's former partner and with whom he made the classic record "The Two Thousand Year Old Man".

Judaism benefitted by the marriage of Elizabeth Taylor to Mike Todd and her subsequent conversion (she was later considered fit by a Reform rabbi to marry Eddie Fisher); and after wedding playwright Arthur Miller, Marilyn Monroe, too, became Jewish, although never acceptable to the Orthodox establishment. She nevertheless enchanted her parents-in-law who were seriously asked if the soup she was given could be made from "any other part of the matzo".

Perhaps the most interesting theatrical conversion of all was that of Sammy Davis Junior – who added Jewishness to his problems of being black and having only one eye – and is proud both of fasting on Yom Kippur and of a son who was barmitzvah. A generation earlier, it would not have seemed possible.

No. Jewish film stars were not really the Jewish studios' bag at all in the great days of Hollywood.

For much the same reasons, they avoided Jewish stories whenever they could. When they couldn't avoid them, they tried their hardest to remove the Jewish content. "Out, out, damn'd spot" could have been the motto of a studio boss faced with a seemingly impenetrable Jewish story line.

Frequently, synagogues in the screen version of successful novels or Broadway plays became churches – for no apparent reason. Plainly Jewish characters with obviously Jewish names found themselves marrying in chapels, such as Dolly Levi (Barbra Streisand) and her newly-found husband (Walter Matthau) in *Hello Dolly* – rabbis became priests or vicars or even doctors.

When Ginger Rogers, Douglas Fairbanks Junior and Red Skelton made *Having a Wonderful Time* (Producer: Pandro S. Berman), based on the Broadway hit about life in the Catskills, every Jewish aspect of the movie was removed and it fell as flat as a matzo pancake on Chanucah.

From time to exceptional time, the studios relaxed their otherwise cast-iron rules. What would *The Jazz Singer* have been without the story of the cantor's son? Yet it was made in 1927 and remade – terribly – in 1953 and once again in 1980 when the climate was altogether different. How *Abie's Irish Rose* or George Jessel's *Private Izzy Murphy* and *Sailor Izzy Murphy* got through isn't quite clear.

When Warner Bros made *J'Accuse* with Paul Muni playing Emile Zola in the story of the Dreyfus trial, all evidence of Dreyfus being a Jew – the whole reason for the infamous case, after all – was removed from the approved story line.

There were, however, fleeting attempts at tackling anti-Semitism (perhaps a fail-safe self-defence move on the part of the moguls) in the late '40s, such as *Gentleman's Agreement* and *Crossfire*, and a slow awakening in a lighter vein through the two Al Jolson biopics, *The Jolson Story,* and *Jolson Sings Again*. In the '50s there was Herman Wouk's family story *Marjorie Morningstar* which had Natalie Wood as the Jewish girl in the title and Gene Kelly, if you please, as Saul Ehrmann that became Noel Airman.

It had a seder service and a barmitzvah (Hollywood Reform style) and was, therefore, a breakthrough.

Exodus was one of a mere trickle of stories about the birth of Israel which would have been a flood about any other country created from such dramatic – and essentially Western – ingredients. *Cast a Giant Shadow* seemed to have it all. The film, starring Kirk Douglas as the American Jewish Major

Marcus who helped the infant state create its army, caused so many problems that its creator Melville Shavelson recalled the experience in his brilliantly funny and sardonic book *How to Make a Jewish Movie*.

When Warner Bros made its classic story of an early concentration camp victim – in the days before anyone knew what a real camp inmate would look like after being subjected to treatment there – *Mr Skeffington* – Jack L. Warner actually asked his (Jewish) director, Vincent Sherman: "Does this guy Skeffington have to be Jewish?" He was eventually persuaded that, yes, he did.

A few years earlier, that very film's writers, the immensely talented twins Philip and Julius Epstein, were told by Warner: "If you'd like to change your names, this might be a good time to do it."

They didn't – and *Casablanca* won them an Oscar in their own names.

Even the Goyishe studios had their Jewish roots.

In the early Hollywood years, William Fox created his own company which later merged with Twentieth Century. William Goetz was production head there. So was Joe Schenck, who had previously been Chairman of United Artists, which was otherwise not a Jewish company. His brother Nicholas became President of Lowes Consolidated Enterprises, which meant that he controlled MGM for some time.

Then there was Hal Roach, who gave the world Laurel and Hardy, and Hal B. Wallis, who was the brain behind Warner Bros – and First National after the coming of sound – and later became an independent producer and senior executive with Paramount.

Barney Balaban, a former head of Paramount, Irving Thalberg the brilliant young man of Hollywood who married the boss's daughter and so (together with his brother-in-law David O. Selznick, himself scion of a top Jewish movie family) gave rise to the saying that MGM was the studio "where the son-in-law also rises" – and Dore Schary who succeeded

Mayer himself, all helped to continue the Jewish domination of Hollywood's boardrooms.

No list of directors could omit the names of George Cukor, Garson Kanin, Fred Zinnemann, Stanley Kramer, Carl Foreman, Jules Dassin, Anthony Mann, Daniel Mann (no relation), John Frankenheimer, Joseph L. Mankiewicz – also an eminent writer – Sidney Lumet, Mark Rydell – after his *On Golden Pond* in 1981 one of the most sought-after directors in Hollywood – Mervyn LeRoy – credited after his *Little Caesar* with Edward G. Robinson with creating the gangster film for Warner Bros – Richard Brooks, Arthur Hiller and, of course, Billy Wilder.

The problem is not where to begin the list but where to end it. But until recently none of them wanted much to make Jewish films.

The holocaust and its camps were not subjects in which anyone had much experience until the '60s and '70s. But the non-Jewish Rod Steiger made *The Pawnbroker* and the world became aware of the Nazi legacy.

True, *The Search* and *The Juggler* had dealt with the problems of the displaced persons' camps and there had been the honourable *Diary of Anne Frank* but it wasn't until Steiger won his Oscar for *The Pawnbroker* that all the gloss was removed and tears, anger and bitterness totally replaced chicken soup and schmaltz.

The gates had finally opened and *Marathon Man* and *The Boys from Brazil*, both dealing – one directly, the other obliquely – with the Angel of Death of Auschwitz, Dr Josef Mengele (both with Laurence Olivier, in the first of which he played the Nazi, the second, the Nazi hunter) proved that nobody was going to be allowed to close them again. The bitterness grew and so did the budgets. Yet from time to time, there was a return to the stereotypes and caricatures which had begun in the '60s with *Goodbye Columbus* and *Portnoy's Complaint*. (In the first, the most tasteless barmitzvah yet placed on record featured the decapitation of a chicken made entirely of chopped liver.)

So Lets Hear The Applause

Britain did things more tastefully with *Sunday, Bloody Sunday* starring Peter Finch, which turned matters around: for once, a story had a Jewish character for no more reason than that he was a Jew.

Jewish show-biz was the essence of *The Night They Raided Minskys;* Jewish nostalgia with a sepia tint in the delightful *Hester Street.* Alan Bates in *The Fixer* told what had to be said about the Czarist pogroms in Russia. And then in the 1980s came Rod Steiger again as the magnificent Chassidic rabbi in *The Chosen* – a world which Barbra Streisand chose for her directing debut in *Yentl,* an Isaac Bashevis Singer story. A Jewish tale very different from the one that formed the basis of *Funny Girl* and *Funny Lady.*

It wouldn't have happened a generation before. Any more than Goldie Hawn would have been allowed to make *Private Benjamin. Private Benson* ... perhaps.

But if there were one movie that made a general box office hit of a Jewish subject, it had to be the 1971 version of the Broadway hit *Fiddler On the Roof.* For once, the prayer shawls were on but you didn't need lockshen soup flowing through the veins to enjoy and sympathise with Topol's aspirations to become a rich man. It was a wonderfully good and entertaining film. And that was enough.

There had been a short-lived Yiddish film industry operating in and out of Poland in the immediate pre-holocaust period, but with the honourable exception of *The Dybbuck,* the films went as they came – virtually unnoticed. When Hitler moved into Poland on 1 September 1939, the Yiddish film went the way of its audience.

The Jewish contribution came via Hollywood or London or occasionally through recent European cinema, as in the brilliant *Garden of the Finzi Continis,* made in Italy with West German help or *The Oppormanns* made in Germany.

Israel's own fledgling film industry has served the Hebrew-speaking public well enough, and occasionally its efforts, like *Salah* and *Rosa,* have travelled abroad. It has also provided occasional facilities for what were termed "Matzo ball

Westerns", like Gregory Peck's *Billy Two Hats,* but these have not proved quite the same sort of money spinners as the crop of teenage sex movies that began with *Lemon Popsicle.*

Show-biz has changed. Like the membership of the Hillcrest Club, it includes as many accountants and advertising men as actors, producers and directors. But these, too, have contributed to the Jewish entertainment story. A story where people have truly believed, in the words of Irving Berlin, "There's no business like show business."

Al Jolson
(1886–1950)

Al Jolson

Let Me Hear Applause – and I'm Happy

Of all the show people who could dominate an audience, Al Jolson stands out as the king. He could not only manipulate the people in the stalls and the balconies, he swept them into his hands as a magnet attracts iron filings. And not just audiences, he taught other entertainers how to perform and three generations of audiences how to be involved in a magical experience.

You didn't just listen to a Jolson performance, you became part of it – often to the despair of those people unlucky enough to be playing in the same theatre or of the men who laughingly were supposed to have written his lines.

Write for Jolson and your work was likely to end in thin air. The words of a script vanished as did the lines of a song, but they always sounded better the way he did them – even if halfway through he would insert a "Dum-dum-dee-dah, get hot" in place of a string of chorus.

When in a nightclub scene in the 1927 *The Jazz Singer* – remembered as the first of the "talkies" – he delayed giving instructions to the bandleader until after the microphones had been switched on, he was merely doing what he had done on Broadway for nearly 20 years. "Wait a minute, wait a minute," he said. "You ain't heard nothin' yet. Wait a minute, I tell yer. You wanna hear 'Toot, Toot, Tootsie'? All right, hold on. Lou, listen. You play 'Toot, Toot, Tootsie'. Three choruses, you understand, and in the third chorus I whistle. Now give it to 'em hard and heavy. Go ahead. ..."

On screen he was ushering in a revolution. Who knows where talking pictures – or, indeed, the cinema – would have been had Al not had those words etched on to wax for posterity? There had been sound sequences in movies as experimental peep shows for years. But whole films – with people talking as well as speaking? In the words of the Jewish Hollywood moguls – "Who needs it?"

It was Al Jolson and a combination of accident and sheer gall – or in Jolson's own mother tongue of Yiddish, *chutzpah* – that sent the silent film on to the top of the scrap heap, and proved that the public did need it.

For years he had been proving that the people who paid the price of admission to a theatre needed him, too.

It was he who at the start of World War One was earning $10,000 a week at Broadway's Winter Garden Theatre, a palace as assuredly his as the residence of any other ruling monarch. In the words of his sometime arch rival George Jessel, when he marched from the stage to his dressing room it was like the procession of a Roman emperor – only this one had been consumed by nerves that twisted his stomach muscles into tangling knots before his triumphant parade.

There was never a case for Jolson to follow convention – because he believed that any worthwhile convention had still to be created. By him.

Jolson's power over an audience was felt on both sides of the footlights. He knew when a sea of ticket-holding faces had warmed to him every bit as much as they knew he was coaxing them to adore him.

Once in Denver, Colorado, Al arrived an hour late for a performance while, outside, the snow was up to two feet deep. Everyone was in his seat, tolerating a supporting company who were as uneasy about being Jolson's warm-up act as the audience were at having to listen to them. Suddenly Al appeared at the back of the auditorium, his coat over his arm, his hat still on his head.

He walked to the centre of the stage and asked: "Do you mind if I put my make-up on now?" They howled their approval. After a non-stop singing performance lasting two hours, Al told them: "Look I'm feeling hungry so I'm going to the restaurant next door, but you can come and join me there.

They've got a swell piano player and when I've eaten I'll sing some more for you." At which point he had boxes of candy passed from seat to seat. Later, the audience crowded into the restaurant and Jolson sang until three or four in the morning.

There were other occasions when he was wrong about his audience. On Broadway one night, the weather was so bad that there were vacant seats in the theatre. Jolson saw them and decided that rather than play to a half-empty house, he would catch the next train to Atlantic City. By the time he arrived, there was a telephone call waiting for him. Jake Shubert was on the line, saying that the crowd in the theatre refused to move until Al came back and agreed to sing. He had no choice but to go straight back and give another early morning performance.

The supreme egoist, this man Jolson, but if he had not been, could he have become such a dominating influence? For Al Jolson to be anything but the greatest – long before a certain boxer was the gleam in his grandmother's eye – was intolerable.

He worried more about the sort of audiences he was likely to meet than anything else. At times he would sit in the box office counting the take. If you dared approach him and ask where the seats were situated, he refused to sell the tickets. You sat where you could get a seat if you were watching Al Jolson!

His only other love was the race track. It was a substitute both for an empty life and for the occasions when he felt even his public didn't love him. He had been known to cancel a matinée so that he could go racing. Equally likely was the possibility of his calling a special matinée – if he thought there were enough people who wanted to see him.

As George Jessel said about him: "Jolson was synonymous with victory. At the race track he would say, 'I had the winner. ... I told you so. I had the winner.' Even if he sometimes achieved that win by backing every horse in the race."

Jessel was equally astute in saying this about him: "Jolson

is the happiest portrait that can ever be painted about an American of the Jewish faith ... For in 1910, the Jewish people who emigrated from Europe to come here were a sad lot. Their humour came out of their own troubles. Men of 35 seemed to take on the attitude of their fathers and grandfathers. When they sang, they sang with lament in their hearts and their voices, always as if they were pleading for help from above ...

"Then there came on the scene a young man, who with a gaiety that was militant, uninhibited and unafraid, told the world that the Jew in America did not only have to sing in sorrow, but could shout happily about Dixie, the night boat to Albany and about a girl in Avalon. And when he cried 'Mammy' it was in appreciation not in lament."

He was above all the consummate Jewish entertainer. Not simply because he sang the occasional Jewish song, but because his whole background and his whole bearing were Jewish, indefinable perhaps, but very Jewish. When he sang his "Mammy" songs – and there were many more than "My Mammy", the one for which he is fondly remembered – he was not so much aping the black man as bringing the style of singing learnt at his father's knee on to the stage.

He was born in perhaps 1886. But it could have been 1884, 1885 or as late as 1888. No one thought about birth certificates in Czarist Russia, and the small hamlet of Srednick was straight out of the stories of Sholem Aleichem and *Fiddler on the Roof*. There, Moses Yoelson conducted services as his father, grandfather and great-grandfather had done before him.

When Asa, his youngest child – he had two daughters, Rose and Etta and another son called Hirsch – was about ten, the Yoelson family emigrated to the United States where before long Moses Yoelson had found himself a job with the congregation at E. Street West in Washington, D.C.

He was employed as the synagogue's cantor, but just as importantly had to fulfil the role of *shochet* – the ritual slaughterer who killed chickens for the use of a community that would never dream of eating anything that was not kosher. Even more valuable was his role as the local *mohel* – the man who circumcised baby boys at the age of eight days, the sign that they were formally admitted to the covenant of the Jewish people.

Three years after their arrival, the children's mother, Naomi, died. It marked the severing of the strong ties that kept the family together.

Asa and Hirsch went on the streets and became, in the word of their father, "loafers". Eventually they ran away from home, changed their names to Al and Harry Jolson and joined up with a crippled vaudevillian called Joe Palmer in an act known as Jolson, Palmer and Jolson. Al's first stage appearance had been as one of the mob in an American version of Israel Zangwill's *Children of the Ghetto*. He even tried to join the troops off to fight in Cuba in the Spanish American war, but was too young even to be a mascot.

It was not long before the two brothers separated, Al to work in a revue, Harry to appear in burlesque where he was featured as the "Ghetto Sport".

Al, meanwhile, was doing very well for himself. A Negro dresser is reputed to have told him that people were sure to laugh at him more if he blacked his face – "because everybody makes fun of the black man". It was a message he took to heart and by 1908 he was singing with the most famous bunch of black-faced artists America had created, Dockstader's Minstrels.

Finally, in 1911, the Shubert Brothers took him to their new theatre, the Winter Garden. They had the presence of mind to ignore the first performance – at which nerves almost destroyed the Jolson career in one fell swoop. Fortunately, the Shuberts were wise enough to guess he was never going to be so bad again. They gave him a second chance at the next day's matinée and watched him dominate the audience like a sheep-dog with its flock.

He had earlier inserted an advertisement in *Variety* in which he said: "Watch me, I'm a wow". That first Winter Garden show, *La Belle Paree*, proved it. The Shuberts followed it with more Jolson appearances and before long had shows written around and starring Jolson himself.

In them all, he appeared in black-face; not to mock the negro but simply because the minstrels were the most popular entertainers on any stage. They were no more making fun of the black man than clowns were ridiculing the white.

But again, it was his Jewish presence that came through.

Despite his family background, he was not religious, rarely if ever went to synagogue, but the songs he learnt with his father stayed in his memory and governed performance after performance.

One Saturday evening in the late '20s he was in a nightclub – as a customer. But the people surrounding his table wouldn't let him just sit there any more than he really wanted to do so himself. They begged him to sing and he was ready to oblige.

But he was not going to give them what they expected. "Folks," he declared, "this used to be my mother's birthday. And because this was my mother's day I'm going to sing a song she loved."

The song was in Yiddish and told a story that was close to his own – about the cantor who went to a small town to audition before the leaders of the community, the *balabatim*, the local tailor, the coach driver and the shoemaker.

The result was a typical Jolson performance. Certainly, Al made a production of the whole affair – singing with alternate sighs and laughs, a deep baritone one minute, a near falsetto the next, and all the time demonstrating how the tailor described the singing as like a fine stitch, the shoemaker as like the finest pair of shoes he had ever created, and the coachman who said it was all as elegant as a royal carriage and as strong as a horse.

George Murray in the *Chicago American* summed it all up: "Jolson made his audience live with him, momentarily, in that far-away ghetto in a tiny Russian village. Having told them what the song was, he sang it. Ben Bernie, who knew the song, accompanied him on his fiddle. Did I say Jolson sang it? It was more than singing. He wept it, he laughed it. It played in his heart and the hearts of all responded to it.

"For 15 minutes or a half hour, Jolson sang the song of his mother's childhood. And in that Saturday night audience, not an eye was wholly dry. There was Jolson, no bigger than five foot six inches, slender, puckish, singing in a foreign tongue of a foreign place."

In reality, Jolson sang most of his songs that way. "You Made Me Love You" – especially the bit saying "Yes I do, indeed I do, you know I do" – was sung as though Jolson were at the reading desk offering a prayer. Without sounding irreverent, he could pack the same energy, the same performance, into the most sacred part of the Jewish liturgy, the Kol Nidre prayer recited on the eve of the Day of Atonement. When Jolson recorded "Kol Nidre" it was placed on the other side of the "Cantor" song.

To Jolson, singing "Kol Nidre", as he did in the first talkie *The Jazz Singer,* seemed perfectly right. It was almost as if he were telling his father: "I haven't left *anything* behind."

In 1948, soon after the establishment of the State of Israel, he recorded the country's national anthem "Hatikvah" and backed that with a rendition of an old Jewish wedding song "Chozen, calah, mazeltov" called, simply "Israel". The lyrics were in praise of the new state. All the royalties went to the United Jewish Appeal.

Jolson was more than anything a *gefilte fish* Jew. He loved the trappings of Judaism without upholding any of its rituals. Above all, he loved gefilte fish. He conveyed that love to his friend Louis Rosenberg, an advertising man, who had his mother present Al with a plateful of the delicacy. After several weeks, Mrs. Rosenberg was still waiting for the return of her plate. "This friend of yours, Jolson," she chided her son, "he likes my gefilte fish so much that he ate the plate too?" By return, Al sent her a $300 bone-china dinner service. He enclosed with it a note saying: "Dear Mother Rosenberg, your gefilte fish was delicious. Sorry I misplaced your dish. Does this make us even? Love, Jolie."

After a time, his own father came to terms with his son the star – even though his brother Harry, ever jealous, never did (probably he didn't like the idea of Al sending a cheque on condition he didn't trade on his reputation).

Al would talk about the cantor in his stage show and on his broadcasts. He loved telling one story that he always swore was true. He had bought his father an overcoat for $200 but he knew the old man would never accept such an expensive gift. So he had the man behind the counter alter the price tag to $12. Cantor Yoelson was delighted. "How did you like the coat I gave you, Pa?" Al asked him a few days afterwards.

"Fine," the old man told him. "It was so good that I sold it to your Uncle Moshe for $30. You didn't know your father was a businessman, did you?"

For years – until the cantor died in 1945 at the age of 95 – the congregation at Washington, D.C. used to revel in their celebrity cantor. I myself have relatives who proudly talk about being married by the older Yoelson.

Jolson's Jewish background had its repercussions in the strangest ways and sometimes in the saddest.

His most traumatic marriage was to hoofer Ruby Keeler. Together they adopted a baby boy, and as far as Al was concerned the baby was the light of his life. He even tried to persuade friends that the child was the spitting image of himself. After a trip to Florida, Al knew the boy would be waiting excitedly to greet him. And he was. Al trundled down the gangplank, picked up the boy and swung him around in his arms. "Who am I, Sonny Boy?" asked Jolson, begging the question.

"You're the Jew," came the fast reply. George Jessel who was with him at the time said that he saw Jolson blanch even under his deep sun tan.

If all the Jewish entertainers sold themselves from a stage, Jolson did so in abundance. He was the ace salesman in a diamond-studded pack. Only he could get up in the aisle of the theatre where Ruby Keeler was dancing and start singing the big production number "Liza". Miss Keeler didn't like it at all,

45

but Florenz Ziegfeld thought it was so sensational a publicity-grabber that he persuaded Al to do it at every show for a fortnight. If he had his way, Jolson would have done the same thing for the run of the show.

Shakespeare said that the whole world is a stage. It certainly was for Jolson. When he went to pay his income tax at the end of the First World War, he was invited to sing for the astonished clerks and the other "customers". One man had his pocket picked as he stood in the crowd – but went on record afterwards as saying that the whole experience made it worth-while.

The most amazing thing about Al Jolson was the recognition he received from his pals. When early this century he started billing himself as "America's Greatest Entertainer", none of his rivals went on record to dispute the claim.

A few years later, "America's Greatest Entertainer" had become "The World's Greatest Entertainer" in capital letters. That was how he was billed on theatre and film posters and even on his record labels – the same label on which were released discs by other stars also labelled "sensational". But Jolson's claim was never disputed.

For years, Al Jolson's greatest rival was Eddie Cantor. Cantor was star of *Kid Boots* and the Ziegfeld Follies while Jolson was the brightest jewel in the Shubert Brothers' theatrical crown. In December 1923, when the snow on the streets of Broadway was deep and crisp and even, Al developed what he said was a terrible attack of laryngitis, and escaped to Florida.

It was in Miami that Jake Shubert found his star soaking up the sun by the side of a swimming pool. Al had a chiffon scarf around his neck, but otherwise appeared to be thoroughly enjoying every ray flooding in his direction. "How are you feeling Al?" asked Shubert. The answer came very quickly. "Terrible," Al scribbled on a pad, "How's Broadway?"

The answer cured Jolson's throat instantly. "Not too exciting," said Shubert. "But Cantor's not doing badly. In fact, he's had his biggest week ever in *Kid Boots*. They took $45,000."

You didn't tell that sort of thing to Al Jolson in a hurry, without carefully weighing up the consequences. "That", he said bristling, "is a damned lie! We must get the next train back to New York .... No .... Find out the first plane."

The result of that match: Jolson–2, Cantor–1.

Eddie once went to see Al do a matinée of his show *Big Boy* in which Jolson played a jockey accompanied by a real-life horse. He said that it took him five weeks to recover from the experience. Years later, the two of them got together for a radio show and ended the performance with a duet of Al's hit "Toot Toot Tootsie". As the orchestra played the fade-out signature tune, Cantor said: "Thank you Al Jolson for the sort of evening only you could make possible. You're still the world's greatest entertainer."

Maurice Chevalier was equally affected when he saw Jolson. "He had punch, you know," he told me, "like the best American entertainers had and which in my own way I tried to copy." Though soon after arriving in the United States, he said, "I felt like getting back on the boat."

Years later, he recorded an album of Jolson songs in tribute to Al.

George Jessel told me over lunch at the Hillcrest Country Club: "Al Jolson wouldn't mail a letter for anyone or do any good to my knowledge, but there isn't anyone who is even twenty-fourth behind him."

Jack Benny was equally forthright – but kinder: "When you talk about the 'World's Greatest Entertainer' you have to say Al Jolson because there was just no one like him. Only Judy Garland and perhaps Frank Sinatra got anywhere near him."

He could sing stirring songs like Gershwin's "Swanee" – a river he was quite 40 years old before seeing – and turn a lullaby like "Rockabye Your Baby with a Dixie Melody" into a military march.

More than that, he could make indifferent songs into great standards – "Avalon", "Keep Smiling At Trouble" and "Baby Face" are typical.

So Lets Hear The Applause

Irving Berlin wrote him a song for the film *Mammy* that became the theme tune for *The Jolson Story*. It was called "Let Me Sing and I'm Happy". Let Jolson sing and he *was* happy. But the title would have been even more accurate had it been "Let Me Hear Applause and I'm in Heaven".

It was said that while others played to an audience Al Jolson made love to it. He did more than that, he consummated his love in public with a passion seen neither before nor since. He wanted to know who his lovers were – so he switched on the house lights of his theatres, just to be certain that he wouldn't miss one expression of their devotion. But a conventional stage was not close enough to the public who were expected to give as much as they received. For their mutual benefit he built a runway to slice the auditorium in two – something that had only been used before as a platform for chorus girls whose physical delights rather than their artistic abilities were on view.

The love affair at the Winter Garden and at any one of the hundreds of other theatres in which Al Jolson appeared was to have a predictable effect. Three of his four wives were to cite an audience as the reason for the break-up of their marriages. The other woman was always sitting in the stalls or in the balcony – and usually in both at the same time.

That was not to say that Al didn't want a stable marriage. "It was easy enough to make Jolson happy at home", said his friend George Burns, "you just had to cheer him for breakfast, applaud wildly for lunch and give him a standing ovation for dinner."

His favourite occupation was taking his wife of the time – or one of the girls with whom he loved to be seen – on to the balcony of his penthouse apartment to look down on the lights of Broadway flickering below. "That's my street, you know," he would say. And it was. Broadway was his from the top of his once curly black hair to the soles of his always shiny black shoes.

Above all else, he craved the admiration of his fellow enter-

48

tainers. An award presented to him by Bob Hope or a ribbing on the air from Bing Crosby were enough to make him happy for days. But at a time when the only people who saw Jolson perform were the ones who attended a live performance, something was inevitably missing. It wasn't easy for a fellow entertainer to see him – because if he were any good he would be working himself.

With that thought in mind – and the prospect of the take at the box office, too – the Shubert Brothers started to organise a series of Sunday concerts at the Winter Garden. The Sabbath entertainment laws were very strict about theatrical shows not showing the same performance on Sundays as on the rest of the week. But concerts without sets or costumes seemed to get round the restrictions. So Al headed what turned out to be a fairly high-powered vaudeville bill.

Appearing with him might be stars such as Sophie Tucker, Fred and Adele Astaire, Ted Lewis and Harry Richman. Occasionally, Al would decide that he didn't feel like singing and take a few weeks off. This usually left the Shuberts in something of a quandary. Who could possibly take the place of Al Jolson? On one occasion, they had the idea of substituting a talented comedian called Jackie Osterman.

Nobody had much hope that Osterman – who as he himself said was no Jolson – would do more than average business. But on his first Sunday might at the Winter Garden he was a sensation. For his second Sunday show every seat was sold, and again the way he controlled the audience was incredible. Jolson heard about his success, too. He flew back from Miami and demanded that Osterman be fired or he would never work for the Shuberts again. It was no contest. Osterman never headed another Sunday night concert bill.

On a different occasion , Jolson waited impatiently in his dressing room for that incredible moment when with one voice the house would acclaim its idol. He edged towards the wings, but could plainly hear a noise that normally only he could create. The chandeliers in the theatre ceiling were positively vibrating – to the sound of another singer. Rosa Ponselle, one of two singing sisters, had come to the end of "My Buddy". In the final chorus, she reached a high note and the result pleased Jolson not at all. He ordered that Rosa be fired. She was; but a few months later was wowing a different audience – at the Metropolitan Opera.

Jolson had had the experience of an opera house himself. In 1918, at the tail end of World War One, he took part in a benefit show at the Met. Took part? As far as Jolson was ever able to take part in anything, he took part. On this occasion as on every other one, he was in charge.

He was due to follow the great Enrico Caruso – who in the words of George Burns who witnessed the event: "wasn't just great; he was the greatest. And this was his own house …."

Caruso had been dazzling the starch-fronted diamond-studded audience who had paid hundreds of dollars to be present that day. He had sung "Vesti la giubba" from Pagliacci and the house had nearly collapsed in wonder. Suddenly, Al Jolson in a crisp blue suit – "he was skinny then", says Burns, this little Jew came trundling on stage, threw out his arms and yelled, "You ain't heard nothin' yet". The people out front didn't know what they were supposed to do. Certainly the opera critics present were far from being impressed. But Jolson was true to his word.

"You ain't heard nothin' yet" had been a promise made and always kept ever since the day in 1906 when in the vestiges of earthquake rubble that had once been San Francisco, he had first discovered the power he had over an audience. From that time on, he used it at every show in which he ever performed.

For other entertainers, to be in a Jolson show was a mixed blessing. On the one hand they were as moved and as proud as anyone who paid for the privilege at being in on a live experience that even today sends shivers down people's spines. On the other, it usually meant that they were consigned to being just part of that audience.

At almost every show, after he had been on stage for half an hour, perhaps even less, he would suddenly dismiss the entire company and invite them all to forget their lines, come out from the wings and listen to him singing.

"Do you wanna hear them or do you wanna hear me?" he would call to the audience. They would always ask for him, shouting in their reply a string of song titles.

And he would never let them down. The magic of a Jolson performance was that he never sang the same song the same way twice. It was an adventure for the audience, but could be sheer hell for the orchestra leader.

He was an innovator on Broadway and in the early years of his career when he had first begun to set records on "the road". The most highly-paid Broadway entertainer of all time suddenly wondered why only people who lived within a cab or streetcar's distance of the Winter Garden should be able to see his shows. He it was who first thought of touring with a New York show. Before long it was the most natural thing in the world for a star to do.

He signed a contract with a near bankrupt studio called Warner Brothers and agreed to make *The Jazz Singer*. The result was not only the end of silent motion pictures, but of vaudeville, too. It also meant – with a couple of exceptions –

that people who would have been also-rans in his Broadway companies could breathe again. No more would he be sending off whole cast loads of performers, nor would he be having other acts fired. (These, incidentally, were not all talented entertainers who secretly yearned to take on the Jolson mantle. On one occasion, he had a team of performing elephants sacked because he thought they were getting too much applause.) No longer would he, in his more generous moods, run the taps in his dressing room – so that he wouldn't hear the thundering applause for people other than Al Jolson.

Was this overpowering conceit? It seemed to be. Larry Adler, however, virtuoso of the mouth organ, who says he was influenced by Al Jolson as much as any full-throated singer, told me he thought that such criticism was totally unjustified.

"You're conceited if you think you are better than you are. Jolson was the greatest. It was an assured knowledge."

He knew he was the trailblazer for twentieth-century entertainment. In the late 1940s when Danny Kaye and a host of other big American names were scoring triumph after triumph at the London Palladium, Jolson turned down an offer to follow their example.

"Everyone's a sensation there," he said, "I like to set records."

Probably even he didn't know how important was one record he set at the end of the 1920s which must now rank as the main Jolson era. He was invited to stand in front of a strange looking contraption in a building in New York City. A few blocks away in another building, people could see Jolson's image on a flickering green screen. He didn't realise that television would eventually all but consume the medium which he had helped to create. But it was another first.

He never thought very much of television at all. He had four sets in his Palm Springs home – it was later to be bought by Frank Sinatra (is there something to be read into this?) – in the early post war years, but he had few ambitions in that direction himself. The talent on the box was not very impressive. In fact, he dismissed it about this time by saying: "It seems that the only thing you have to do to appear on television is to show up."

This was an error in judgment – something that happened from time to time. An example of this was his decision to stay on in Hollywood after *The Jazz Singer* – a story mirroring his own career; about a cantor's son who chooses the stage and a black-face act instead of the synagogue and a set of canonicals.

He was made to measure for *The Jazz Singer*. The following year, he made a picture in which baby love was substituted for mother love. So far so good. The movie *The Singing Fool* was a sensational success. In fact, it was not until *Gone with The Wind* ten years later, that the box office records were broken. As for the theme song, "Sonny Boy", it became the world's first one-million and then the first two-million seller for a popular tune – yet another Jolson record. He had rung the songwriting team of De Sylva, Brown and Henderson and told them he wanted a song for a little boy who was dying, a number full of all the sentiment he could get.

The song writers couldn't take him seriously and turned out "Sonny Boy" as a joke, draining from it every drop of schmaltzy sentiment they could produce. When they finished, they were so ashamed of their work that they couldn't bring themselves to mail it to Jolson – they took the coward's way out and asked the page boy at their hotel to post it for them. But it became the hit to end all hits.

His judgment had worked fine so far and why should it now fail? He followed *The Singing Fool* with *Say it with Songs* which was about another little boy – played, as it so happens, by the same kid as in the earlier film, Davey Lee – and now he had "Little Pal" instead of "Sonny Boy". It was written by the same team and even more dreadful than the first song. Both film and song did reasonably well, but were not in the class of their predecessors.

Before long it seemed that the incredible talent called Al Jolson had created a monster that was about to consume him. He showed moments of genius in *Big Boy*, the film of the Broadway show – simply because that was what it was, a film of the art of which Jolson was king. You could all but sit back in your seat and imagine being overpowered by the magic of the Winter Garden. But you can't film a magnetic field and neither could you encompass Jolson's magnetism in a movie.

Within ten years he was down to playing third lead in two films for Twentieth Century Fox, *Rose of Washington Square* and *Swanee River*. When he could play Al Jolson himself doing what Jolson did best, singing Jolson songs, he was spellbinding. But opportunities were limited.

Had the Japanese not invaded Pearl Harbour, that might have been the end of the Jolson story. He could have died leaving a couple of obituary paragraphs in *Variety* and some of the heavier newspapers, but little else. However for once his judgment was right.

He became the first American entertainer to volunteer to entertain the troops. Suddenly, for a limited audience, Al Jolson was bigger than ever. He had found his finest hour.

On a lonely street corner in Alaska or in a mud hole in Italy, he would approach a group of homesick G.I.s and say, "My name's Jolson and I sing – do you wanna hear me?" They always did.

Suddenly, the word went round that this dynamic "new" singer called Jolson was giving the sort of shows that they had only read about. The kids – and to use Al's phrase about another group of soldiers, "they really are kids" – were expecting Bing Crosby and were hoping for Lana Turner. Instead, they were left with memories that would be with them all their lives. And with their families too. Back in the States, Al sat himself down with a telephone for company and started dialling numbers: "Mrs. Schwartz? Hello, Sammy sends his love. Sang to him in Africa last week. Sure, he's feelin' swell." "Oh, Mrs Murphy? I was talking to your Michael yesterday. Yeh ... in Alaska. My name? ... Al Jolson."

He was working harder than ever before and enjoying every minute of it. A couple of years earlier he and Ruby Keeler had divorced, and a succession of beautiful girls was not nearly enough for the man who above all wanted to hear the sound of tumultuous applause.

Once more people were worshipping Jolson the entertainer and it was a religion he wanted to promote. It could have gone on for as long as the war itself had Al not been struck down by a combination of two highly dangerous diseases: the first, audience fever, the second a bad bout of malaria.

In the end, he collapsed, had a portion of his lung removed and found that his voice – if he had the strength to use it – was four keys lower. Strangely enough, this made it all sound warmer and better. Certainly, that was the belief of the patients at the Service hospital which he toured once he regarded himself as better – his doctors did not think he was ready for more than sitting by his swimming pool, playing a bunch of old Jolson records.

At one of those hospitals he met a 21-year-old X-ray technician called Erle Chenault Galbraith, offered her a job in pictures and then married her.

In the meantime, Al had also become a Hollywood producer. It was not exactly a spectacular landmark in his career. He used to joke: "I had an office with couches and beds in it. For months, nobody called me. One day, the phone finally rang and I answered all excited. A voice said, 'Is that Shapiro, the plumber?'"

It was rather like Al's relationship with Erle. He was happier at home now than he had probably ever been before. For once there was a Mrs. Jolson who did not have to compete with a screaming mob. But he was restless. It was one thing to show his new wife his scrapbooks, quite another to show her first hand just how he made those old chandeliers rock.

When friends came in for cocktails he would buttonhole them on the quiet. "Tell Erle," he would say, "Tell her just how great I was."

Finally, the phone in his office rang and the voice at the other end wasn't after a plumber. It was Hollywood columnist Sidney Skolsky who had been trying for years to sell the idea of a film about Jolson's life to any studio that would listen. At last, Columbia bit. The result was history. A three-month production schedule was doubled, the film was shot in technicolor, lusher orchestrations and extra numbers were added and it paid off incredibly.

With *The Jolson Story*, a whole new generation found a new Al Jolson. All his old dynamism and his magnetic power over an audience returned. Erle could not only see for herself how great he had been, but how great he still was. In a popularity poll, Jolson at the age of 64 came out ahead of Bing Crosby, Perry Como and that upstart Frank Sinatra.

It was the most spectacular comeback in history, and was followed by a sequel that did almost as well. That was called *Jolson Sings Again* – although in truth he had never stopped since he first realised he could open his mouth and produce notes.

What Jolson had above everything else was style, and part of his style was that he was completely unpredictable. In the two biographical movies, Larry Parks mimed the songs while Jolson himself sang. The trouble was that, as in the live theatre, he sang the songs differently at every rehearsal and at every "dry-run" before the cameras and the microphones were switched on. Parks was never sure which version he was going to be expected to mime.

He was a powerful show-biz figure – and a tough man to cross. While making the first film, he had pushed a wad of dollar bills in front of a musician who had had the audacity to suggest that an earlier version of "April Showers" sounded better than the one he was singing now. "I made this in show business," said Jolson. "What have you made?"

He had once thrust a file of papers into the hands of songwriter Sammy Cahn. He told him: "I bet your friend Frank Sinatra will never have anything like this." "This" was his stockholdings, headed by 10,000 shares of AT and T.

As Cahn says in his own delightful book *I Should Care*, Sinatra now has his own folio of shares, including doubtless a nice number of AT and T.

Al Jolson

Yet it was at a party given by Morris Stoloff – the musical director who updated most of the arrangements of the old Jolson songs to make them sound new again in the two biographical films – that Al sang his heart out and was congratulated by a young man who was asked to sing, too. "I can't follow that," said Frank Sinatra and walked away.

Jolson was happier than he had ever been. If he believed that there was still something missing in the way of a challenge, the invasion of South Korea by the North in 1950 put paid to that.

From the Pacific came an irresistible call, the plea of an American Serviceman saying: "Come and sing to me."

The journey first to Tokyo then to Korea itself took days. Jolson arrived nursing a badly infected throat and for the first time really looked his age. His most memorable performance was in a swimming pool where he "gave out" – to use one of his own favourite phrases – with songs like "Swanee" and "April Showers".

As he told Louella Parsons in a short-wave radio broadcast: "The kids loved every minute of it. Oh, what a ham I am!"

That ham arrived back in the States – again using his own words – "two shakes ahead of a fit". He wasn't sleeping well, his pulse was racing and he looked as bad as he felt. But an institution called Jolson couldn't sit on his backside remembering the successes of the past – even the recent past. He accepted an invitation from Bing Crosby to appear on his radio show in San Francisco on 24 October 1950.

It was a date he couldn't keep. The night before, playing cards with a bunch of cronies in his suite at the St. Francis Hotel, Al clutched his chest, whispered "I'm going, I'm going," and died.

The incredible thing is that the Jolson legend and the power that went with it did not die. He is remembered today while pop stars of mere months ago are forgotten.

His records still sell in abundance – barely one has been deleted from the catalogue since they were made in his comeback years of 1946–1950 – and his fanclub is one of the strongest anywhere.

So Lets Hear The Applause

But his most important legacy is the number of people who still say that Al Jolson was their greatest influence – singers as different as Tom Jones and Frankie Vaughan, Eddie Fisher and Tony Bennett. Not forgetting Larry Adler and his mouth organ.

The now few contemporaries still remaining think of him nostalgically and with not a little touch of jealousy. But most of them would give anything to see that man jump on to the runway and shout: "Folks, you ain't heard nothin' yet."

Chico Marx
(1887–1961)

The Marx Brothers

Chico, Harpo and Groucho (and not forgetting Gummo and Zeppo)

Anarchy Unlimited

At one time there were five. Now they are all gone – in life that is. But in memory, in tradition they won't be forgotten. They are a show business institution. Their influence in the history of screen comedy was tremendous – so much so that it is impossible to encompass their story in a few brief pages. This is merely token recognition of what they stood for.

No one will deny that *the* Marx brother was the one born Julius. To any cinema buff, to anyone who likes to smile to himself sitting on a train or at the wheel of his car, that man spelt satire, comedy professionalism in golden capital letters. That man was of course Groucho Marx.

Mention the name and the memory evokes a man with a painted-on moustache, pacing the room as be bends forward like a swaying tree trunk. From the twisting mouth comes a staccato phrase like: "I never forget a face – but in your case I'm prepared to make an exception." Stupid puns like sending his moustache in the post by "hair mail". Ridiculous asides to the cinema audience that kill any pretence of the drama being serious. Rude comments to the huge but strangely pretty Margaret Dumont who struggles in vain to preserve her dignity as he assassinates every scheme she tries to initiate.

Groucho became the unofficial captain of the team known as the Marx Brothers. Under him, going their own way to inevitable anarchy, were the rest. Such as Harpo who never said a word but strummed a harp with an angelic look on his face and called attention to himself with a car horn, and with a wardrobe that the Salvation Army would have put into the incinerator.

Only his brother Chico was able to understand the intricate mimes perpetrated by the "dumb" Harpo. Chico, meanwhile, played tricks on the piano keyboard and, in an age when every man thought he could get ahead with a hat, wore a bonnet and spoke with an accent surely left him by an Italian organ grinder.

Just occasionally in the early films, there was an irritatingly normal-looking brother who always seemed to get in the way of the comedy and who never sang as well as Allan Jones or looked as pretty as Kitty Carlisle. His name was Zeppo.

Earlier still in their career they had been joined by a gentleman called Gummo, but he threatened to literally gummo up the works and took another role with the "family firm".

To some people, seeing a Marx Brothers film was almost a religious experience. Winston Churchill, for one, was a devoted fan. It was he, after all, who refused to interrupt a showing of *The Big Store* – the film in which Tony Martin introduced "A Tenement Symphony" – to hear the news of the flight of Rudolf Hess to Scotland.

Nor should it be forgotten that George Bernard Shaw once said: "Cedric Hardwicke is my fifth favourite actor – the first four being the Marx Brothers."

Their story begins in a tenement on 93rd Street in New York City. In those days, their main task was to try to divert their neighbours' attention from the remarkably inept tailoring of their father, who was quite the least skilled man who ever took up a needle and thread.

It was their mother Minnie, born in Germany to a family named Schoenberg, who kept the family together. Her husband Sam however always managed to look well dressed (he obviously had better sense than his customers) and was nicknamed "Frenchie". The kids were pretty good with nicknames

Harpo Marx
(1888–1964)

– as their careers in show business later demonstrated. An uncle of theirs was called the General.

At this stage, therefore, it does not go amiss to introduce the correct dramatis personae: Chico was really called Leonard, Harpo was Adolph (later and before becoming Harpo he was called Arthur), Groucho was Julius, Gummo was Milton and Zeppo was Herbert. (As the family became more American-ised their taste in names became more localised.)

Chico was born in 1887, Harpo a year later, Groucho in 1890, Gummo seven years after that and Zeppo, the baby, in 1901.

Harpo today is remembered as possibly the nicest and kind-est of the Marx Brothers. While the others were always trying to top one another's jokes or their women, Harpo sat back happily enjoying being entertained. He was probably the most literate of the brothers – as his letters to Alexander Woollcott, if not his ghosted biography *Harpo Speaks*, demonstrate.

Chico was usually broke.

Gummo, who had at one time sold ladies' clothes, stayed on as the brothers' business manager for years after they stopped performing as a team. But he kept the particularly unique Marx Brothers sense of humour. When Groucho underwent an operation in the 1950s, he told a reporter: "The operation was so minor that Groucho would have done it himself if only he could have got someone to hold the mirror."

Zeppo joined the act after working for a time for the Ford Motor Company. He never really liked show business and, when the time seemed ripe, decided to switch to making money from other people's talent. He worked both as manager for the other brothers and as an agent. But he could be devastatingly funny and on occasions actually substituted for Groucho. To judge by later sayings of the brothers they did not appear to be desperate to be together too often.

They owed a great deal to other people's humour – and not just the ones who paid to laugh. S. J. Perelman, who wrote a number of their screenplays, deserves much of the credit. But the brothers were never mere mouthpieces for someone else's joke factory. They did more than deliver other people's lines. Anything they ever said could easily have come out of their everyday conversation, and frequently did. If Groucho never actually left his place at a restaurant table to address the other diners with an aside or stop the passers-by on Hollywood Boulevard to give a commentary on a traffic jam, you always knew he could do so at any moment.

Groucho's wit could be murderous. He was once asked if he thought the tunes of George Gershwin would be played in 100 years' time. "Sure," he said, "if George is here to play them."

His conversation was usually of the bluest – and not always in private. In the days when those shows were live, he startled a television contestant – not to say a few million viewers – by his reaction to the news that she had 13 children. The woman told him she loved her husband. "I love my cigar," said Groucho, "but I take it out once in a while."

In London he told a fawning restaurateur that he would never go to his establishment again – "because I don't like the sort of place that would have me as a customer."

It was Groucho Marx who was credited with telling the beach club that refused him membership because of his faith: "My son's only half Jewish. Would it be all right if he went into the water up to his knees?" (Groucho's son, Arthur Marx, reports this in his book *Son of Groucho*, although to be fair, Al Jolson once said a similar thing when Harry Richman was refused admission to a golf club.)

In his book, Arthur Marx says: "Father is not anti-Semitic. He admires Golda Meir. He gives generously to all the Jewish charities. He is what I'd call an anti-Jewish chauvinist."

Maybe Groucho's greatest achievement was that names like Otis B. Driftwood, Rufus T. Firefly and Dr. Hugo Hackenbush are almost as well known as his own – which, of course, was not his in the first place. Perhaps only a Marx Brothers devotee could really explain that one.

Their mother Minnie was the one with stage ambitions. Her brother had changed his name from Schoenberg to Sheen and had joined up with a gentleman called Gallagher. Further

Groucho Marx
(1890–1977)

description ought to be superfluous, but let it be said that to anyone who had ever been inside an American vaudeville theatre or who knew someone who either had or had read about someone who had, the phrase "Oh, Mr. Gallagher ..." automatically brings the rejoinder "Oh, Mr. Sheen".

Brother Al's success inspired Mrs. Marx to try her luck with her boys – and since Frenchie wasn't bringing in too much wealth from making a pair of pants with legs of different lengths or jackets that happened to have only one sleeve, he could not but agree. Mama Marx, hereinafter called Minnie, was aiming at more than just bringing in some money. She was positively stage struck. She really had little reason to be so. Her mother had played the harp while her father had been a magician in Germany. He was never very successful and would often follow the word "magic" with another – "schmagic" ....

Groucho had been put into an act as a boy singer but, after being relieved of his money on the road, formed an act with Harpo. It flopped like the pants of a burlesque comedian. It was Minnie who decided that something had to be done. She put all the boys together, called them The Four Nightingales and went back on the road – playing not just mother to her brood but manager, too. All except Zeppo, that is; he was still too young.

Notices appeared in the local papers:

Miss Minnie Marx
presents the
4 Nightingales 4
The only juvenile quartet in vaudeville

When that failed, Minnie brought in Zeppo and her own sister Hannah, at that time destined for an operatic career. The nearest she got to that was as part of an act now known as the Six Mascots. Frenchie and the General went along for the ride selling clothes en route with about as much success as the rest of the family were having "on the boards".

Their activities were so spectacular at that time that a critic wrote: "The Marx Brothers and their various relatives ran around the stage for almost an hour. Why, I'll never understand."

Meanwhile the boys were running from town to town, too — as much to get away from the alternate enthusiasm and disgust of local womanhood as from the critics. They had seen the temptations of low cut bodices and flesh coloured tights and had succumbed. Minnie for her part was more concerned with finding customers than with her sons' prospective suitors.

In Texas, they decided the time had come for yet another new name: The Marx Brothers and Co. It sounded rather like a chain store and before long the "and Co" was dropped, but finally in those years immediately after World War One, they were making an impact. They didn't always appreciate the finer points of Texas patriotism, however. "The jackass is the finest flower of Texas," said Groucho at one show and the boys were chased out of town after all of them had sought refuge in the first-aid box.

It should be added here that one of the original four Marx Brothers to go on the stage under that name wasn't a Marx brother at all. Chico had left the family act and gone to work as a salesman for a firm of music publishers, and his place had been taken by a kid called Lou Levy. Before deciding to rejoin the brothers, Chico gave up the publishing business and went on stage as a single, as pianist. For his first performance, he covered his face in rouge. The manager asked him: "What are you playing, Indian?"

Before long, the brothers were together with a new act called Fun In Hi Skule. One of the most notable features on this were two signs, one marked "BOIZ", the other "GOILS".

Like most people starting out on a new career — certainly the vast majority of those in show business — the Marx Brothers and Minnie were constantly in debt, sometimes more because of Mrs. Marx's poker losses than any lack of offers.

But Chico always seemed to owe more than the rest of the clan put together and this had been so for as long as anyone could remember. Indeed, Harpo got so fed up with his elder brother constantly hocking his favourite barmitzvah present, his watch, that he decided to put an end to it once and for all. He took off the hands.

Yet suddenly they found themselves booked on the Orpheum circuit, one of the biggest in vaudeville, and earning $900 between them – big money even when it had to be divided six ways and more.

Minnie was their manager for a very long time but even when she had grown old and after she had died, to some vaudevillians the brothers were still known as Minnie's Boys.

What was very obvious at this time was the bond inside the family and particularly between the brothers, sometimes taken to ridiculous lengths. When Groucho had an operation for appendicitis, all the other brothers were present as the surgeon tried to bring him round from the anaesthetic. It was a primitive age and Groucho had been given ether. The only way the doctor knew of waking him up was to slap his face. When the brothers saw this, they slapped the doctor.

It was the sort of anarchy that delighted audiences. In his charming early Marx Brothers biography, Kyle Crichton says that they played the famous Palace so often that they became known as the theatre's stock company. And the Palace was as high as a vaudeville act could ever hope to climb.

They even took the act to England and learned to cope with the different tastes of British audiences. After a poor start – in which the audience threw coins on the stage and Groucho appealed for silver – they became favourites all over the country.

And so it went on. Until an Irving Berlin show called *The Cocoanuts*. They had had previous legitimate experience in *I'll Say She Is*, and *Too Many Kisses*, but *The Cocoanuts* established them as stars who looked as though they were here to stay.

They even made a silent film called *Humorisk*, but fortunately for them they had a serious moment of thought long enough for them to decide to buy up all the copies and never allow it to be released.

They stayed with the stage and a new show *Animal Crackers* provided them with as much success as had *Cocoanuts*.

The coming of talking pictures made them think again about films. Had they not done so, the Marx Brothers could have been among that long list of has-beens known only to the oldest oldtimers and historians of vaudeville. Instead, the two words *Duck Soup* have become a legend.

It was a notable Hollywood first – soon both *Animal Crackers* and *Cocoanuts* became films, too, and were followed by *Horse Feathers, Monkey Business, Room Service, A Night at the Opera, A Day at the Races, The Big Store, A Night in Casablanca* and *The Marx Brothers Go West*.

About the time of *Cocoanuts*, Alexander Woolcott decided that Harpo ought to start thinking about some real culture. He sent him tickets for Shaw's *Arms and the Man*. Since he would have to dress up for the occasion, Harpo thought better of it and gave the ticket to Frenchie. Mr. Marx Senior grabbed the opportunity – after all, he did so much like putting on tails and a stiff white shirt. He arrived at the theatre before anyone else and spent the time until the arrival of his fellow patrons looking around the building and talking to ticket sellers, ushers and the doormen. When people started arriving, Frenchie appointed himself official guide to the theatre and gave each one a lecture on the quality of the architecture, the comfort of the seat and the artistic merits of the performance they were about to see. He was so convincing that by 8.30 he had talked himself into believing it was all too cultural for his own tastes and went home.

Quite obviously the father of the Marx Brothers was as much a character as were Chico, Harpo, Groucho, Gummo or Zeppo. In *A Night at the Opera* he persuaded them to allow him to be an extra. The only trouble was he was in the same sequence twice – on the quay waving goodbye to himself on a ship. The brothers decided not to tell the MGM boss, Irving Thalberg, who was largely responsible for creating the success that gave birth to the Marx cult.

So Lets Hear The Applause

One of the big problems about all of their films was not just the way they made confetti of their scripts, but the effect that had on the picture and, in turn, on their audiences. No one could ever be sure how a Marx Brothers film would end until shooting finally finished. What the scriptwriters produced and what the directors had decided was entirely irrelevant. The name Marx Brothers became so synonymous with anarchy that they took advantage of this and tended to treat a picture like a string of spaghetti – which never came to an end. The films generally climaxed with a one-liner from Groucho that had to be pulled from another part of the picture.

The last film by the brothers, *Love Happy* with Marilyn Monroe in 1950, was but a shadow of their previous glories, but was good enough to satisfy the Marx nuts and please an ever more sophisticated movie audience.

By that time, Groucho had his successful radio quiz show "You Bet Your Life" which later switched to television; Harpo settled down to become a devoted family man; Chico gave much of his time to cards and women, and the other brothers seemed to be dividing their interest between women, business, women and women.

Chico died in 1961 and Harpo three years later. Groucho continued to appear on television and to do a series of one-man shows. In the early '70s he was still making appearances, much to the dismay of his most devoted fans. He was not even a ghost of his former self as he shuffled around, usually wearing a beret, and almost always accompanied by a pretty girl.

In 1976, Zeppo's ex-wife married Frank Sinatra. Zeppo and Gummo were mostly intelligent enough to keep themselves to themselves. In 1977, Gummo died. Within months, Groucho was dead too. The next year, Zeppo followed them. They were the Marx Brothers. Nothing more needs to be said.

Barbra Streisand

The Way She Is

It may not be easy for either herself or her detractors to accept
the fact, but Miss Barbra Joan Streisand is a throwback to a
past age. She is still in her early forties, still has her name in
lights, still makes new record albums and still attracts cameramen like wasps to a jam jar. But everything about her smacks
of The Generation.

Born in Brooklyn in 1942 with the second "a" in her name,
she was brought up with the smells of gefilte fish and schmaltz
herrings filtering through the walls of the apartment house at
Pulaski Street. She was left fatherless as a baby, became stage-
struck as a teenager and was a star at 21.

She is not only a magnificent performer, but a hustler in the
tradition of a Jolson or a Tucker. The fact that she did it
playing for much of the time essentially Jewish roles is not
entirely coincidental.She wouldn't like it said – and anyway it
would not be strictly true – that she needed to mimic a woman
in a Lower East Side kosher butcher's shop before she could
succeed, but it has added a dimension to her character that she
might not otherwise have had.

She might not even recognise it herself, but when she sings
"My Buddy" or "The Way We Were", she is almost leading
her audience in prayer as though she were a cantor in the midst
of a congregation. The words of her song matter as little as
those chanted in the synagogue. It is a question of "feel".
Singing those ballads she can take an audience with her
wherever she wants to go. Lamenting about being a Second-
Hand Rose on the other hand, she brought back a style of
ethnic humour that purists had hoped had been dead for 20
years. The fact that she was doing so while playing a previous

"great" Fanny Brice, turned out to have little to do with it. Probably fewer than one in ten would even have known that the song also was second-hand.

It is a measure of her success that she could play Fanny Brice without being frightened that it would swallow her – as playing Al Jolson overwhelmed Larry Parks. Her biggest triumph, however, is that she is both a good actress and a powerful singer in an age when solo singers are rare, and many performers, some with poor voices, join a rock group to get into the charts.

There was no reason to expect that the baby born to Emmanuel and Diane – née Rosen – Streisand in April 1942 would go into show business. The couple were young and had the familiar Jewish dream of going places. They could have been *children of* The Generation themselves. Emmanuel didn't come home from a tiring day pushing his cart through the crowded street markets, planning the sort of education he never had himself for his elder son Sheldon and the baby Barbara. He was already a Ph.D. and a teacher. The sky seemed the limit for his family – once the war was over and he could really extend himself.

Just over a year later, however, that dream ended. Emmanuel died of a cerebral haemorrhage. He was 34.

Before long, Diane married again and had another daughter – who would also try her luck in show business – and Barbara felt increasingly out in the cold. She also found a way to overcome that feeling – by becoming an exhibitionist. As a young teenager she wore the most outlandish clothes that the second-hand stores offered. She would walk down the street with ladders at the back of her stockings – the fronts were all right, so if she couldn't see them herself, what did it matter? Not an unusual Jewish trait that.

It was when she saw a performance of *The Diary of Anne Frank* that she decided there and then that she wanted to be an actress. If she couldn't get acting roles, she wanted to sing. She even cut a demonstration record, but it was worn out on her own record player rather than on that of any producer.

So Lets Hear The Applause

Leaving school, she sang in "gay" bars and helped at theatre workshops. She even managed to play a part in a small theatre near Albany, New York. The play was *Teahouse of the August Moon*. She rode a goat from one end of the stage to the other.

Most of the rest of the time, she was washing up in a Chinese restaurant. And she didn't have much of a social life, either. Her mother had warned her never to hold hands with a boy – which tended to limit the number of dates she received.

She decided, however, that the time had come to branch out. And the first thing to do was get herself a new name. She hadn't thought about simply dropping a letter from her own. She looked through the Manhattan telephone book and came up with Angelina Scarangella. She thought that way she could keep the name Barbara Streisand pure for when she was a star. Let Angelina Scarangella do the suffering.

Singing a song called "A Sleepin' Bee" – which for a time was the lynchpin of her repertoire – she won an amateur talent contest and thought that stardom was hers for the asking. But she still had some asking to do. Yet before long she was featured at the Bon Soir nightclub singing a number of brand new songs. She got them by telling publishers she was the secretary of Vaughan Monroe, a top pop singer of the age, and would they kindly let her have some complimentary sheet music?

There was a word for that: chutzpah. But even chutzpah can't carry an artist for ever. Talent took over when cheek, of necessity, faded.

She was paid $108 a week. Angelina was almost ready to become Barbara again. When she decided that the time had finally come, she couldn't quite face her public without something of a disguise. So Barbara became Barbra. It was enough of a deception to let her come right out in the open without a serious bout of nerves. Jack Paar, then a leading TV host, gave her a spot, and this was followed by a series of appearances on a popular programme called "PM East".

What separated Barbra Streisand from the others was a little thing called *I Can Get It for You Wholesale* – the New

74

York rag trade, Broadway style. She was one of dozens of aspiring hopefuls who auditioned for the role of Miss Marmelstein, the secretary in a clothing firm. She walked away with it – and particularly with one number, itself called "Miss Marmelstein". Time magazine said it was "the only bargain in an evening that was otherwise strictly retail".

The part was very much a good buy. The little Jewish girl with the large Jewish nose was a sensation. But that nose did worry *Variety*, the show-biz "Bible". "Get it fixed," the paper suggested. She decided not to do so. She was not religious, knew only a few Jewish expressions, but that nose was her link with her heritage.

A couple of years later when – against the explicit advice of producer David Merrick – she landed the role of Fanny Brice in *Funny Girl*, there was something strangely attractive about her. She seemed to be saying "Jewish is beautiful" when she pranced on stage in a whole wardrobe of outfits that ranged from an outrageous baby style to a figure-hugging silk suit.

Funny Girl was a strange show. But like "Wholesale" the strangest part of all was that it depended solely on Miss Streisand, then a rounded 23 who neither looked nor sounded very much like Fanny Brice. Indeed, although Miss Brice used to use Yiddish accents on stage that were so coarse they made new immigrants feel refined, she rarely spoke like that at home. In *Funny Girl* in 1963, Barbra used them all the time – and with telling effect both in her lines and her songs, particularly when she describes a gourmet's paté as chopped liver.

The Jewish intonation – making even the most dogmatic statements sound like a question– was never more tellingly used than when she talked about her appearance. "What do you think?" she asks the boss of a vaudeville show who fires the young Fanny Brice, "beautiful girls are going to stay in style for ever?" There had to be variety. What would happen if shops only sold onion rolls and in walked a bagel? "That's my trouble. I'm a bagel on a plate full of onion rolls."

It was a bagel that rolled round the stage of the Winter Garden Theatre and on a good night could earn a succession of standing ovations. On other nights, she would try for a whole different interpretation and leave everyone feeling rather like the matzo pancakes Fanny Brice's mother used to make. On still other occasions she allowed a steadily expanding reputation to carry her – and it dropped her on her behind.

She took the show to London while she was pregnant. Some evenings the reaction of the audience was as big as her stomach. On others, the customers were tempted to ask for their money back.

Her then husband Elliott Gould whom she met in the "Wholesale" show – where he played the male lead – often complained he was treated the same way. In her early days of success, before he, too, became an international star, they lived in a smart Manhattan apartment and every day would begin with his cooking the breakfast and then calling, "Barbra, come and get your chicken soup." But they drifted apart.

Barbra, meanwhile, was on to other things. Her record albums were instant sell-outs, each one of them showing a greater sensitivity and an increasing sense of style, and always with the plaintive sound of cantorial chant about them.

She sang before two presidents – Kennedy and Johnson – and then worked to get Senator McGovern elected in the year that Richard Nixon won his landslide election victory.

On reading the first reviews of *Funny Girl*, a lingering sense of insecurity overcame the ovations. "Will somebody tell me," she kept asking, "am I great or am I lousy?"

Later on, there would be a sense of the superstar about her. The girl who used to love to wear outfits bought at church sales (the synagogue sales were too smart) suddenly appeared in the best-dressed woman lists. Interviewers – if she spoke to them at all – would be put down with caustic comments or given precise instructions about pronouncing her name properly. "It's Strei-sand. You rhyme it with Dry Sand."

By that time, she had made a number of big films and the occasional big turkey. The first was a screen version of *Funny Girl* – which was successful enough to be followed six years later by *Funny Lady*, which took Fanny Brice completely untruthfully to old age. Whereas *Funny Girl* had dwelt on Fanny's love for the gambler crook Nicky Arnstein, *Funny Lady* concentrated on her marriage with (and then divorce from) Billy Rose. The real Miss Brice had described him as "the most evil man I know", but Barbra played her as always carrying a torch for him.

In between the two pictures, she achieved a stunning comedy success in *The Owl and the Pussycat*, made two of the funniest pictures of the '70s – *What's Up Doc?* and *For Pete's Sake* – and the charming *Up The Sandbox* and *The Way We Were*. This last was about a girl not unlike Barbara Joan Streisand from Brooklyn who falls for a WASP who happened to look a lot like Robert Redford.

At one time she planned to star in a film about that other Jewish entertainer, Sarah Bernhardt, but decided to settle for Fanny Brice.

There were also two big musicals, *On a Clear Day You Can See Forever* and *Hello Dolly*, both pleasant in their way, but now liable to send show business accountants into near hysteria.

On a Clear Day suffered because Barbra was miscast as a young girl who finds herself back in another age. The trouble was that it wasn't the right age for Barbra Streisand. Somehow, you couldn't imagine the girl from Pulaski Street wearing a mob-cap and living in Regency England.

Hello Dolly in 1969 had Barbra Streisand aged 27 playing the widowed matchmaker Dolly Levi – in the trail of Carol Channing, Mary Martin, Ginger Rogers, etc., etc. Unfortunately there was a distinct lack of chemistry between herself and Walter Matthau, the tight-fisted bachelor she is supposed to woo.

Matthau once described her to me – despite some difficulty in getting the words out – by saying: "Barbra Streisand is the most... the most ... extraordinary ... er ... uninteresting person I have ever met. I just found her a terrible bore. But very nice. One day, I had an argument with her. It was very hot and sticky and Bobby Kennedy had just been assassinated. I was feeling rather blue and hot and I just screamed at the person who was nearest to me – and it happened to be Miss Streisand.

"She was doing something and asked the director if I wouldn't mind saying my lines a certain way. I think I said something to her like: 'I was acting before you were born – so please don't tell me how to act.' And she said in her own inimitable way: 'Is this guy crazy or something?'"

Everything about *Hello Dolly* was crazy. Not just the casting, but the timing, too. It lay on the shelf a cool two years so that every ounce of paper money could be swooped up into the box offices of Broadway, Chicago, Los Angeles and London before mere cinema audiences could see it.

The fact that Barbra Streisand could recover from *Hello Dolly* says more than a little for her own talent.

Probably her real recipe for success is that she has stayed Barbra Streisand – if always a little more so, cultivating her own gauche personality as film follows film. She once apologised to Princess Margaret for being late for a party saying: "I got screwed up on the way."

When she heard that the Arabs were protesting about the Egyptian Omar Sharif playing Nickie Arnstein in *Funny Girl*, she said: "You think Cairo was upset? You should see the letter I got from my Aunt Rose."

Doubtless, her aunt Rose has been following her career avidly ever since. She might even be persuaded to see her niece, the producer, at work. In that role she made yet another version of *A Star is Born* – this time with Kris Kristoffersen playing a pop singer with herself stepping into the satin slippers vacated first by Janet Gaynor and then by Judy Garland.

In 1983 against practically everyone's advice, she became a film director and starred in the movie, too. It was *Yentl*, an Isaac Bashevis Singer story about a girl who disguises herself as a Yeshiva student. She filmed in London and Czechoslovakia and researched it by living among the Chassidic Jews of London's Stamford Hill, going to their weddings, witnes-

78

sing their bereavements. It was another milestone; something she had to do.

What makes Barbra run? In 1964 she told *Time* magazine: "I had to go right to the top or nowhere at all. I could never be in the chorus, know what I mean? I had to be a star because my mouth is too big. I'm too whatever-I-am to end up in the middle. The exciting part has been trying to get to wherever it is I'm going. It was exciting to get kicked out of all those casting offices."

She has been at the top now long enough never to be kicked out again.

Danny Kaye
(born 1913)

Danny Kaye

Court Jester

When Al Jolson died in 1950, one eminent student of the world of the theatre wrote: "Who now becomes the World's Greatest Entertainer? I can think of only one possible successor to the title: Danny Kaye."

In 1950 it was a logical conclusion. He seemed to have all the magic, all the personal magnetism and dynamism that Jolson had had, all the sheer brilliance that makes a distinctive performer.

In short, Danny Kaye was outstanding. He was not just a great entertainer in 1950 terms, but *almost* a genius. Looking back now with the benefit of hindsight and some knowledge of the show-biz industry more than a century ago, the appellation still seems partly justified. Of all the people who were topping the charts and commanding large fees, Kaye is one of the few who is still remembered and who is still identifiable. Perhaps of those stars of a generation-plus ago, only he, Fred Astaire and Frank Sinatra (and until his death, Bing Crosby) would still merit a full-scale photo call at the airport, a cluster of radio and TV people ready to drop anything for the chance of an interview.

The difference is that Astaire and Sinatra are still producing – whether it be records or stories about themselves. Kaye, though younger, is not. Danny Kaye was always more than a good actor or singer. He was a master entertainer – a court jester (to coin a film title) who could turn an auditorium into fairyland; a comedian who made a visit to a cinema become an occasion when you needed a bottle of embrocation lotion to ease your aching sides.

He had such a command of the English language and could

manipulate words so skilfully that even the most dedicated adherents to the tongue of Shakespeare would find themselves doubled up with laughter.

But the work that he performed magically suddenly stopped. It wasn't that he wanted to retire while "on top", before age and the fickleness of public taste took its toll. He suddenly decided to change course. He had had enough of doing what people expected – and wanted – him to do. It seemed that he had turned his back on being an entertainer.

He is a very good dancer, but his dancing is at its best when he dances as much with his hands as with his feet. And this act we haven't seen for almost a generation.

He can't read a note of music, but that does not stop him conducting the world's top symphony orchestras. All right in its way. A highly talented thing to do – but why stop? No satisfactory explanation has ever been offered.

He has no medical diploma either, but he would love to have been a great surgeon. Friends say he can converse with the most eminent members of the medical profession in their own language. He has been known to put his medical knowledge into practice. Once he kept a woman suffering from a heart attack alive for the length of an aeroplane flight.

He could also have become a chef – specialising in Chinese dishes. But instead he became an entertainer and we ought to be glad that he did. Why, though?

"It was something I had to do," he has said. "A man usually becomes what he has to become rather than what he wants to be."

While it is surely everyone's right to make his own decisions – and he has had time to devote himself to some marvellously worthwhile causes – the loss to his one-time devoted public has been great.

He is a Walter Mitty man, just like the character he played in one of his most brilliant films – one minute a surgeon, the next an RAF pilot, then a mariner saving his ship and all sailing in her from the perils of the deep. And all the time, as in the story, his mind and his ambitions race, te-pocket, te-pocket, te-pocket.

He has always been brilliant when talking to children. He would tell stories that not only made them laugh, but which also made sense. He never talked down to the kids. He paid them the compliment of speaking to them on his level. Myer the Cryer wasn't just a tearful boy in hospital, but one of *us* who quite naturally didn't like being away from home. Only Danny Kaye could be a Cryer like Myer – pulling faces like an india rubber man and holding his breath like some piece of complicated machinery.

In his way, he made everyone feel like a child – with himself as Santa Claus and his performance as the present.

The children have been luckier than the grown-ups. For them he has continued to sing and play – most often going round the world for UNICEF, the United Nations Children's Emergency Fund, an organisation that has virtually become his own charity.

As a result of his first expedition on behalf of UNICEF he made one of his most moving films, *Assignment Children*.

He once said in a BBC radio interview: "It has been the most rewarding and satisfying thing I have ever done. It has accomplished a great deal and that is something I am very comfortable and happy with."

If anyone spoke an international language, it has been Danny Kaye's communication with children. Children in Korea. Children in Africa. Children in Israel and children in Los Angeles.

"One of the failures of communication between adults and children", he says, "is a very simple one. Most adults are too inhibited to behave like a child when they are with children. I've never had that kind of inhibition. Children have radar built into their heads. They can sense whether you really like them or whether you are pretending to like them. And when they do that, there is no way you can turn on a kid or turn him off. They turn you off like a click, the minute they sense you are pretending."

84

He likes telling the story of his daughter, Dena – as in his song, "Deenah, is there anyone feener, in the State of Caroleenah ..." – who, when she was about four years old, was asked by one of her father's friends: "What's the matter, sweetheart?" and she replied: "I don't like you."

Society demands, he says, that we should train our children not to say that sort of thing. Yet Danny Kaye was very much the centre of High Society.

In 1948, at the age of 35, he had taken the London Palladium by the strings of its curtains and pulled down every old tradition that the theatre had known. It was the most incredible triumph London had seen. The King and Queen came to see him and so did the two Princesses, Elizabeth – the present Queen – and Margaret.

It was about this time that Dena was heard weeping her heart out in her father's dressing room. A kind-hearted wardrobe mistress came rushing to the little girl's aid. "What's the matter?" she asked.

"It's all those people," Dena replied, "I don't like them always laughing at my daddy."

That laughter paid for Dena's every want, but it was never more than just a fair exchange. For what Danny gave – sometimes after having to be literally pushed on to the stage after an attack of nerves that threatened to completely consume him – was almost priceless.

There were not many children in those Palladium audiences. But they went to see his films – some, such as *The Court Jester* itself and *Hans Christian Andersen*, were made very much with children in mind. And for children he recorded songs that remain unequalled, "The Little White Duck", "Popo the Puppet", "Tubby the Tuba" and, from that huge collection of numbers from the Hans Andersen film, "The King's New Clothes" and "The Ugly Duckling".

In many ways, the children's songs replaced his tongue-twisting scat tunes as Danny Kaye's trademark. His reason for dropping one in favour of the other is very much like his decision not to repeat his television series of the mid-1960s. "I don't want to do the same thing again. But if there is another *way* of doing them ... fine!"

It is not just nostalgia that makes one wish he would think again about that. True, he could do things nice and easy – to quote from one of his nice and easy songs "Ballin' the Jack" – just by sitting on the edge of the stage and talking to the audiences. But when he got into one of his mad frenzies and sang-talked about the Nazi spy with the unpronounceable Teutonic name, he was doing what only Danny Kaye could do.

You may yourself have thought about the craziness of watching a big film with its strings of opening credits following on ice cream commercials and trailers, but only Danny Kaye could make a classic comedy routine out of it. "Manic Depressive Pictures Present ...", from his very first film *Up in Arms*, has become a classic.

And only Danny Kaye could take the name Tchaikovsky and turn it into a song – with verses that were otherwise mere names from the pages of a Who's Who of Russian Music.

"There's Malaichevsky, Rubenstein Arensky and Tchaikovsky, Sapelnikoff, Demitrieff, Tcherepnin Kryjanowsky ..." It went on through 50 more names, all of which sounded so much better sung by Danny Kaye than in print.

And then there was "Anatole of Paris" – who said ... "let me get my paw on a little chapeau – at 60 bucks a throw."

Many of those words came, not from Kaye himself, but from his wife Sylvia Fine. He has described himself, in fact, as a "wife-made man", which is only partly incorrect. She was the daughter of the dentist in Brooklyn for whom Danny worked as an odd job boy. He was about 14 when she first met him. In those days, Danny Kaye was David Daniel Kaminsky who sang and joked with some of the toughest kids in New York, in the Brownsville section of Brooklyn. He was born in January 1913, son of Russian immigrants. His father, Jacob, had been a horse dealer in Ekaterinoslav, but now in the New World they were going to have to learn to do another kind of horse dealing in the broadest sense of the term, that is – every man for himself.

He did his first acting on the stage of his Brooklyn school, PS 149, after convincing his parents that they could, if they tried, get to understand a different language from Yiddish.

At one time, he considered being a boxer, but he wasn't really built for it. He compromised by taking up table tennis – and became ping-pong champion of Beverly Hills, but that was to be a generation and a career away.

His first professional entertaining was in the early years of the '30s. And he chose the best apprenticeship ground that the entertainment industry could then offer – the Borsht Belt. In the Catskill Mountain resorts, he was a "toomler" – his principal job being to stop the guests becoming bored. If they didn't remember his name after a show – and Kaminsky was a difficult name to remember – that didn't worry anyone but him.

Then he went to Japan and almost ended up in prison. He had arrived at just about the time that the local Musicians' Union had decided they had had enough of American visitors, and he was constantly being barracked – and worse.

In 1939, he came to London, scene of what was to be his biggest triumph. He imagined he was going to be a huge hit in 1939. But he wasn't. Playing in cabaret at the Dorchester Hotel he was an absolute disaster.

A year later, he married Sylvia Fine, who determined to make something of him. As he was to say not so long after that: "She was a great head on my shoulders."

He began to resent Sylvia's influence, and for a time they went their separate ways, but there was no doubt that he did better with her than without.

Early in the war, he played in a show called *The Straw Hat Revue*, which didn't amount to much. But then he was featured in a Gertrude Lawrence vehicle on Broadway by Kurt Weill called *Lady in the Dark*. He was so sensational in the show that the next day he was given featured billing.

So Lets Hear The Applause

He had a brilliant nightclub booking at La Martinique which hit all the headlines and he then went on to sock 'em dead, to use the in-phrase of the time, at the Paramount Theatre. As he went on stage for the first time, he was greeted by the sound of pneumatic drills working outside the theatre.

"Never mind the cannon, fellas," he said, "just tell 'em I'm glad to be back." Ad-libbing Danny Kaye had found his true place.

That was followed by *Let's Face It*, which put him so firmly on the Broadway map that he could never be completely removed from it. The memory of Danny Kaye singing Sylvia Fine's "Melody in 4F" is enshrined together with Jolson's first "Mammy" and Chevalier's "Louise".

It was the head of the William Morris Agency, Abe Lastfogel, who suggested that Samuel Goldwyn should come to New York to catch the Kaye act. As a result, Goldwyn brought Kaye to Hollywood and after failing to persuade him to change the shape of his Jewish nose settled with turning his red hair blond. The outcome was *Up in Arms*, which in turn led to *Wonder Man* and then to *Walter Mitty*. Danny Kaye was at his finest – to use what at the time might have seemed an unfortunate phrase. Danny was coming more and more to resent Sylvia Fine's influence.

They may have been helped somewhat by the arrival of Dena, who saw her father in action for the first time when she was about five.

She sat in the audience as her father called out, "Dena are you out there, honey?"

She called "Yes" – and burst into tears. As for Sylvia, she said in 1947 that she was going to write a book about her marriage called "Seven Years in a Pressure Cooker", but never did.

London in 1948 gave Danny Kaye his greatest triumph. When he and George VI were pictured together, caption writers were not altogether off the mark by calling it a meeting of two kings.

Winston Churchill was just as much a fan as the King. He

called round to Danny's dressing room at the Palladium. "It's a good thing you're not a politician", said the great statesman, now in Opposition. "You have a tremendous grip on a crowd and would be a formidable adversary in politics." And he praised the Kaye approach to an audience when he turned away momentarily, paused and then with proper timing put the greatest possible emphasis on the next few words. "Yes, it's a good trick. I first used it myself on a speaking tour of Canada. I picked it up from Otis Skinner."

While he made his Goldwyn pictures and gave perform-ances such as the one at the Palladium he was king of every-thing he approached. But then he decided to broaden out and do ... well, perhaps not enough. His films for other companies were never very good. *Hans Christian Andersen* made a lot of money but was not Kaye at his best, although he has always liked it very much himself. His own favourite role was the first he did without music, *Me and the Colonel* in which he played a very dignified Jewish refugee escaping from Poland with an aristocratic Polish Army officer. Had he made more pictures like that, his change of direction would have been more universally applauded. But he wanted to do more and more different things, with the result that nobody really saw him doing what he did so much better than anyone else.

But in 1954, the film industry acknowledged an undoubted debt to Kaye – by awarding him a special Oscar for "his unique talent and services to the film industry and the Ameri-can people."

He has always been a man of principle – sometimes earning the undying cheers of one section of the community to the disapproval of another. In 1967 after the Six Day War he broke his contract to play at Britain's Chichester Festival so that he could fly to Israel to entertain the troops. Certainly in Israel he has shown himself as the emotional Danny Kaye, Kaye the Jewish entertainer. But there has been too little of the Kaye most of his admirers grew to love.

There is the occasional bright spot in this story. In 1971, Kaye played the role of Noah in a Richard Rodgers show *Two by Two*. The show lasted for over a year – a year in which Danny drove Rodgers to the verge of despair. Kaye broke a leg and when he returned to the show, used the leg as a prop with which to indulge in his own kind of clowning – much to the delight of his fans. Every night he would do something different, usually in a wheelchair. In the end, audiences were provided with the first piece of genuine Danny Kaye clowning they had seen for years.

There have been too few opportunities to see him in recent years, although he did star movingly in 1982 in a TV film about victims of the holocaust called *They Marched Through a Thousand Towns*. The following year he underwent major heart surgery. In 1984 he was planning a London comeback, in the stage version of *Cage aux Folles*. He is one of those entertainers who come once in a lifetime. Fortunately, he came in mine. Other people have cooked Chinese meals, conducted symphony orchestras, performed brain surgery. But there has been only one Danny Kaye.

Eddie Cantor
(1898–1964)

Eddie Cantor

Making Whoopee

If Al Jolson was the World's Greatest Entertainer – and he certainly was – then Eddie Cantor has a right to compete for the number two slot. And if Jolson is still remembered, still imitated, still almost a household name (if not a cult) almost 34 years after his death, surely Eddie Cantor, who died only in 1964, must still be remembered and honoured.

Things have not worked out quite that way. Jolson's greatest attribute was that he learned how to get round the generation gap, to mould his style according to the period and to succeed in having two films made in what he would like to have considered his image. Cantor was always the Ziegfeld star who danced just a little too much for later tastes, and whose high voice was ideal in the '20s and '30s but was already sounding dated at the beginning of the '40s. He, too, had a film made of his life story – produced by Sidney Skolsky who had produced *The Jolson Story*, directed by Alfred E. Green who had directed *The Jolson Story* – but there the similarity ends. An unmitigated disaster, *The Eddie Cantor Story* did nothing either for the image of Cantor or for posterity.

He deserved better. He was undoubtedly one of the most outstanding men who ever trod an American stage. What is more, he made some of the most popular films to come out of pre-war Hollywood, went on to become a radio star without peer and to have an enviable following on television. He was also a character, in the broadest show business sense. And when Al Jolson considered Cantor his greatest rival as he most certainly did he was bestowing a great compliment on him.

92

Cantor did a great deal, too, for Tin Pan Alley. "Margie", "If You Knew Susie", "Makin' Whoopee" and "Yes, Sir That's My Baby" were as much his property as "Mammy", "Sonny Boy" and "Swanee" were Jolson's.

Above all, he had a style that was uniquely his own. He danced from one end of the stage to the other as though he were taking charge for the evening. (It also implied a sweeping away of everyone else who dared face the footlights before he did.)

When he moved his hands first from side to side then across his chest he was selling his act every bit as much as the newsboys outside the theatre were selling their papers. And when he sold, audiences bought. A Cantor show that was anything but a sell-out was unheard of.

He is also remembered, in contrast to Jolson, as a good man by almost everyone who knew him – if a little on the tight side.

One story has it that a fellow actor down on his luck, went to see both Jolson and Cantor. Jolson looked the man over, wrote a cheque for $500 and berated him for being a "no-good bum". The man left, clutching the cheque and hearing Jolson ball out: "I don't know how you could get into that condition! You're a bum!"

Cantor, on the other hand, kept his cheque book to himself. "Oh, you poor fellow," said Eddie, "go and see Gus Edwards and Ziegfeld and tell them I sent you." Neither Edwards nor Ziegfeld was able to help, and Cantor didn't spend a penny, but for years the actor was saying: "Jolson is a dirty rotten bastard. But Eddie ... what a gentleman!"

He may not have regularly put his hand in his pocket but there was usually a kind word for a fellow performer in trouble. There was always work and sympathy for his fellow Jews. He might even have deserved the reputation as the Best Jew in Show Business. Straight out of the New York East Side ghetto, he never either forgot his roots or was reticent about them. He appeared on Zionist platforms at a time when it was unpopular to do so. He raised money for Israel Bond drives when others were still hesitating, and in 1948 said he would never allow any of his films to play in a country that was anti Israel.

Before that, he raised huge sums for Jewish refugees from Nazi Germany. Non-denominational charities, like the fabled March of Dimes, could depend on him too, and there was always an Eddie Cantor boys camp going somewhere.

Above all, Cantor was part of the very fabric of The Generation.

He was born in 1892 as Isidor Iskowitch – his parents died when he was still a baby and his most formative years were spent under the guidance of the woman he called "Bobba", his grandmother. It was partly to help Bobba keep their home going that he entered his first amateur vaudeville contest.

He decided very early on that he wanted to go on the stage and that Eddie Cantor sounded a better stage name than Isidor Iskowich. At first jobs were hard to find.

He found one as an office boy with the National Cloak and Suit Company. But he failed to keep it when the boss discovered he had lost the firm's collection of postage stamps.

He worked as a singing waiter on the Bowery and again in Coney Island – where he was accompanied by a youngster called Jimmy Durante. At the same time he doubled as a "plugger" for the next-door shooting gallery.

His first real stage job was in a burlesque show called *Indian Maidens*.

The big break came when he was 18 and went to work for the famous Gus Edwards and joined up with a ten-year-old youngster called George Jessel who even in his eighties was about as precocious a performer as you could imagine.

At that time, Cantor had been doing whatever work he could get on a stage; just, in fact, to be on a stage at all. One week he could be working as a Yiddish comedian, the following one singing as a black-face minstrel, sometimes giving imitations of big stars of the day such as Eddie Leonard.

Edwards was looking for an act called "Benches In The Park" and needed someone to play a tramp. Cantor looked at young Jessel, said he would make a lovely baby in a pram and informed the impresario that he himself had been living with tramps all his life. Later, he and Jessel formed an act called Kid Kabaret. But he still continued doing impersonations – including one of a man who to date had never heard of the young Cantor, Al Jolson.

Before long, Jolson caught the act – and went back to Cantor's dressing room to congratulate him. That was no mean achievement in itself.

With another young performer called Sammy Kessler Eddie went to London in 1914 for the Andre Charlot show *Not Likely*.

He was described as a "typical Moroccan", the nearest the British at the time liked to get to talking about black-face. The show "died", but it was then that Cantor thought of adding a pair of lensless glasses to his make-up.

This act finally broke up at about the same time as Eddie married his childhood sweetheart Ida. It was to become one of the happiest of show business romances. While many marriages within The Generation appeared to crumble, the Cantors' stayed firm – through the Depression, a change in public taste, a couple of serious heart attacks and the birth of five daughters, about whom he would talk incessantly on his radio shows. The five daughters became characters in their own right. They also proved a financial headache. He and Ida had made what they considered to be a perfect arrangement for the inevitable. Eddie would leave his money to Ida and Ida's would go to the girls. As things turned out, Ida died first, the money went to the girls and Cantor was left virtually stranded.

But let's get back to where that money originally came from – Cantor's immense fund of talent. It also came in no small measure from a pair of huge eyes which he could make travel in any direction virtually independent of each other. The eyes, the dancing hands and the scar down his forehead from a childhood injury became his great trademark.

One of his most popular acts was playing a chauffeur – in black-face, as were most of his early routines – and reciting a whole succession of off-colour jokes. He made 15 entrances and exits, in each of them displaying another distinct Cantor quality – a perfect diction that could be understood and heard as clearly at the back of the house as at the front.

Among those who heard him and laughed and applauded with the rest of the audience – a rare thing indeed for this man – was Florenz Ziegfeld. He offered young Cantor a one-night tryout at his New Amsterdam Theatre on Broadway. The year was 1917 and Eddie Cantor almost literally brought the house down. There were very few players who could make the walls rock and Cantor was one of them.

He became the sensation of the Ziegfeld Follies. He even made the men out front forget the near-nude girls on stage, a tremendous feat. As for the women, they loved this little figure whom they felt they could take to their bosoms without it seeming to be a sexual act.

With Cantor on stage, there was no need for the splendid costumes and scenery that distinguished a Ziegfeld show from any other. Even so, relations between Cantor and Ziegfeld were frequently strained. The great showman resented the way Eddie sided with the vaudeville artists during the famous 1919 performers' strike. He disliked even more the way Cantor seemed to help along the romance of two of his stars, Jack Carter and Marilyn Miller, the girl for whom "Ziggy" was prepared to throw away an empire.

He, therefore, forbade Cantor to perform in any benefit shows put on by other managements. On one occasion, he heard that Eddie was about to break that ruling and went along to see for himself. Cantor meanwhile heard about the Ziegfeld plan. In the middle of his act, he broke off to walk down to the front of the stage and advise: "Mr. Ziegfeld, it's not me you see up here!"

Later, they would warm to each other considerably. Cantor was one of the few of his comedians whom Ziegfeld found funny. In 1923, he persuaded him to star in a "legitimate" musical show, *Kid Boots*. Eddie drove up for the meeting with Ziegfeld in an outrageous check golf outfit complete with huge cap. The showman was so taken with this that he persuaded Cantor to wear the outfit in the show – in which he played a caddy – and it was to be one of the most popular Cantor routines of all. It was in this show that Eddie introduced the classic number "Dinah".

Ziegfeld never believed in telling anyone to do anything face-to-face if a telegram could do it for him. During the run of *Kid Boots* he sent Cantor a 12-page wire, suggesting changes. Cantor replied with a telegram of his own – containing just one word: YES. Ziegfeld was furious. He sent another telegram: WHAT DO YOU MEAN YES DO YOU MEAN YES YOU WILL TAKE OUT THE SONG OR YES YOU WILL PUT IN THE LINES OR YES YOU WILL FIX THAT SCENE OR YES YOU HAVE TALKED TO THOSE ACTORS.

Eddie's answer: NO.

Kid Boots was followed by another Ziegfeld smash, *Whoopee*. Both became films.

When Cantor developed laryngitis, Ziegfeld sought out the top throat specialist in Pittsburgh to attend him. The only problem was that the doctor had himself just had a near-fatal car crash. Ziegfeld went to the doctor's home, pushed past his nurses and wrote a $1,000 cheque to persuade the man to paint Cantor's throat. The $1,000 was too much to resist even for a patient on what appeared to be his death bed. He was taken on a stretcher to Cantor's hotel room where he painted the infected throat and prescribed the necessary medicines. The $1,000 was well invested. Eddie recovered.

Eddie's grandmother was undoubtedly the big influence on his life and remained so even when he became a Broadway star. She fell seriously ill just as he was making a big name for himself with Ziegfeld. Will Rogers walked into his dressing room one night at the New Amsterdam Theatre to find Cantor weeping like a baby. A short while afterwards he told Cantor at a 1922 Friars Club dinner in his honour: "That's what makes you a regular fellow to me. There's a gag along Broadway that all of us Christians have a pet Jew. You're mine."

The experience of the 1919 strike stood Cantor in good

stead with his fellow performers. For years afterwards, he was called in by Equity to act as arbitrator and peacemaker in a whole succession of suits – including one that threatened in 1939 to bring the career of Sophie Tucker into oblivion. He was most loved by the show people who were his contemporaries. But even he could be ruthless in the stories he told about them. When George Jessel was earning himself a reputation for his young brides, Cantor went to the microphone at the beginning of a show to apologise for his friend's non-appearance. "Jessel couldn't get here tonight," he said, "because his wife is teething."

His entry into films was swift. As early as 1911 he had had a screen test at the behest of Gus Edwards.

Then in 1926, he made the (silent) film version of *Kid Boots* for Paramount in which he co-starred with Clara Bow. It took in a lot more money than the movie he made for the same studio the following year, *Special Delivery*.

But it was the coming of sound that made him an international celebrity. He had appeared in a couple of talkie shorts before *The Jazz Singer* made his rival Al Jolson the most important star of the age. But it was after the silent picture had become a museum piece that he decided to make Hollywood his home.

In 1929, he filmed *Glorifying the American Girl* which had always been Ziegfeld's philosophy in life. Ziegfeld gave the picture his own blessing and allowed his name to be bandied about as if the whole thing was a giant publicity exercise – which it probably was.

Whoopee was made in 1930.

His films, if figures published in the *Motion Picture Almanac* were to be believed, attracted huge audience figures and brought in amazing sums to the box office. But the *Almanac* commented that the figures were "supplied by Mr. Cantor himself".

In 1931 he made a film called *Palmy Days* about a candy factory. As a result of that, he became one of the first Goldwyn musical stars – signed on a five-year contract with Sam Gold-wyn's studio to make films like *The Kid from Spain*, in which he played a comic bullfighter, *Roman Scandals*, in which he imagined himself back in the days of Caesar, and *Kid Millions* and *Strike Me Pink*, both of which featured a young Ethel Merman.

In 1938, he starred in Twentieth Century Fox's *Ali Baba Goes to Town* and moved to MGM for a big flop called *Forty Little Mothers*.

Three years later he was back at the place where he still felt most comfortable, Broadway, in a show called appropriately enough – *Banjo Eyes*. But he returned West again for *Show Business* with Joan Davis and George Murphy in 1944, and for the 1948 film *If You Knew Susie* – also starring Joan Davis – which partly cashed in on Al Jolson's comeback. It did a lot more good for him than *The Eddie Cantor Story* in 1952, which had Keefe Braselle doing very unsatisfactorily what Larry Parks did so brilliantly for Jolson.

In fact some might think that *The Eddie Cantor Story* had the reverse effect on its subject to that of *The Jolson Story*. Internationally, it seemed to pull down the curtain on his career. It didn't actually do that. At the time, he still had a radio programme and an occasional TV show, too.

What really happened was that time had begun to take its toll and Cantor joined the ranks of the hundreds of enter-tainers who still made a very nice living thank you without being plastered all over the front page of *Variety*. Towards the middle of the '50s he became ill and never recovered.

But the entertainment industry remembered him. In 1956 he was awarded a special Oscar and just before his death in 1964 President Lyndon B. Johnson awarded Cantor a Medal of Freedom. He was too ill to receive it in Washington, so the award was presented to him on the lawn of his own Beverly Hills house by George Jessel. A few weeks later he was dead.

Completely self-educated, he was an amazingly literate man and wrote three autobiographies: *My Life Is in Your Hands* in

1928; *Take My Life* in 1956, and *The Way I See It* in 1959 and a book of reminiscences, *As I Remember Them*, published the year before his death.

Eddie Cantor may not be popular today but no history of the American theatre can present him as anything but a headliner.

Edward G. Robinson
(1893–1973)

Edward G. Robinson

Big Little Caesar

Edward G. Robinson was never just an ordinary actor. Nor was he most people's idea of star material. When he screwed up his face to smile, he resembled rather an advertisement for lemon squash.

As the years advanced, that face looked more craggy than ever, but a grey beard added a mark of distinction. Added a mark of distinction? Well perhaps that is an unnecessary statement. For Edward G. Robinson was himself a mark of distinction, a man who added a dignity to the screen and – perhaps rivalled only by his fellow Warner Brothers contract artist Paul Muni – was the most distinguished Jewish film actor of all.

I met Edward G. in what might be described as the twilight of his life. He was already very deaf and the dark brown age spots on his face indicated that he would not be playing very many more roles. Thereafter, seeing him in a cinema was an experience to relish rather like sampling an old wine that you know can never be repeated.

We talked about the changing cinema, the changes that had come since the days when he was "Little Caesar" going down to his death, clutching his heart and saying: "Mother of God, is this the end of Rico?" Perhaps not the sort of epitaph that the small boy who came from Romania to America as Emanuel Goldenberg would have expected.

He had done a great deal since the Warner studio moguls had wooed him from the Broadway stage to become one of the focal points of their gangster picture era. But he insisted that his philosophy of acting had not changed.

"The changes are not all that noticeable. There is a certain dramatic intelligence that guides you. As the screen gets wider and the soundtrack gets louder, your own pace should guide you. The thing is, you should not be bothered by the machinery. You have got to have talent."

And that is something that Edward G. Robinson always had.

But it was a special kind of talent. The kind that made you feel sorry for the crook because you knew that behind that tough exterior was a real man with a heart and soul. I remember weeping a silent tear every time I saw him succumb to a bullet. And when he was arraigned in court for a banking swindle or a con trick that went wrong I just knew that there was some hidden force driving him to an end he had never really deserved.

How could he do that?

"You have to be a person on your own," he explained to me then, sitting in a gigantic suite at London's plush Claridges Hotel. "You have to be able to assume the externals of your role and bring out the human qualities.

"It's what you do after you stop being a gangster that counts. You have to get to the inner man and bring him out."

It was a talent he always had, although early on in life he really had no more idea of being a film actor than he had of muttering the words "Mother of God". If he were going to speak out, he decided shortly before his barmitzvah, it would be from the pulpit. For young Emanuel Goldenberg dreamed of becoming a rabbi.

He was born in 1893 the fifth of six sons and had gone to America only after the older three of his brothers had tested the lie of the land and decided it was free of most of the anti–Semitism from which the Goldenbergs had suffered.

His ambition to become a rabbi waned and he decided that he wanted to become a lawyer. "Always a defence lawyer. I never wanted to prosecute."

He had discovered his talent for projecting his voice and stating an unarguable case in club debates and what were known as "declamation contests".

Finally, he decided to become an actor – although he said his mother never really felt as glad about that as she was about the achievement of his younger brother Max. He became a dentist.

Years later, however, his love of his parents became his only real religious affiliation, although he was always an ardent Zionist. Every Yom Kippur, wherever he was, he would go to a synagogue and recite kaddish.

In the early years of the century, however, he didn't think of that. Only of making a name for himself. It was very early on, in fact, that he made that name. While still in drama school, he called himself "Edward G. Robinson" in a play called *Bells of Conscience*. He was the star. As he says in his own autobiography, it did not happen again for another 15 years.

In the years between, he established himself in a repertory company and in one play took two roles – listed first on the programme as Edward G. Robinson and for the second role as Emanuel Golden.

Finally, at the age of 29 in a theatre in Denver, Colorado, he was billed not only with his name above the title but with his photograph on the cover of the programme.

Soon after that, he made a silent movie in Cuba called *The Bright Shawl*. (He saw himself in the film at a matinée, whilst he was engaged in the production of *Peer Gynt* by the most famous American repertory company of them all, the Theatre Guild.)

He made a success while he was still young, virtually a Broadway star by the time he was 30. When talking pictures came, Warner Brothers were not alone in trying to bring him into their orbit. But Broadway was not a place you ran from lightly. It was every actor's goal and to give it up and go to that place where they made the "flickers", Hollywood, was almost a betrayal of one's heritage, even if your father did come from Romania and was still a junk salesman.

Robinson had been playing in a play called *The Kibbitzer* and had then gone to San Francisco in another called *The Racket*. It was the first time he had seen California and he loved everything about it – but decided he did not want to stay, despite offers, he insists, from every studio in Hollywood.

But he made a film for Walter Wanger in New York called *Hole in the Wall* co-starring Claudette Colbert.

Finally, he was persuaded to go to the movie capital to take part in a picture for MGM called *A Lady in Love*. No sooner had that been wrapped up than he made one for Universal, *Outside the Law*. That in turn was followed by *Widow from Chicago*, a resounding hit.

Producer Hal Wallis was as impressed as everyone else and before long he was making *Little Caesar*. The rest, as they say, was history.

For the record, that history included such outstanding pictures as *Barbary Coast*, *Kid Gallahad*, *A Slight Case of Murder*, *The Amazing Doctor Clitterhouse*, *I Am the Law*, *Confessions of a Nazi Spy*, *Brother Orchid*, *Tales of Manhattan*, *Double Indemnity*, *The Woman in the Window* and *Our Vines Have Tender Grapes*.

My own taste – and taste is always a subjective thing – tells me that 1948 was probably vintage Edward G. Robinson year. He made what I think must be his two best films ever – *All My Sons* with Burt Lancaster, a moving Arthur Miller story about a man caught up in the groundswell of war-time moneymaking, and the classic Humphrey Bogart/Lauren Bacall co-starring venture *Key Largo*.

But then something happened. Robinson was yet another of the Hollywood crowd to become a victim of Senator Joe McCarthy – but in a somewhat unusual way.

In a report of the UnAmerican Activities Committee, he was listed as a member of what were claimed to be several Communist-front organisations. There was no dispute that he belonged to them all – although he did hotly deny they were Communist or red-inspired. In fact, he said he did not know how anyone proved he was not a Communist. But the groups bore names that McCarthy regarded and thought other people would regard as Communist – names such as the National Congress on Civil Rights, the American Committee for Protection of Foreign Born and, worst of all, they said, he was a leader of Progressive Citizens for America.

Other Hollywood people lost their jobs after being mentioned by McCarthy. Warner Brothers did not go as far as breaking their contract with Robinson, instead they made him suffer – while continuing to pay him. The name Edward G. Robinson continued to appear in their cast lists – but in low-budget second features.

He never again starred in his own right in an outstanding major film. But he did make a comeback, taking second and third leads, and played a handful of memorable cameos. Altogether he made another 31 films – including, most notably, *The Ten Commandments*, *The Prize*, and *A Hole in the Head*. He also appeared on television, shortly before his death in 1973.

As a collector of art treasures, he earned an international reputation of a different kind. But when his art collection is forgotten, the impact he made by the brilliance of his acting will be remembered. His was a talent of the kind one says: "We will not see his like again." It was an immense talent – as perhaps it had to be. As he told me himself: "Considering my size and my looks – I ought to be an encouragement for anyone."

Jack Benny
(1894–1974)

Jack Benny

A Pat and a Pause

I first met Jack Benny when he walked through the lobby of the plush Plaza Hotel in New York, a tired look on his face and a violin case in his hand.

Somehow or other, those two features have come to symbolise Jack Benny, born Benny Kubelsky in 1894 in Chicago – although he would always tell anyone who wanted to listen (and he was one of those entertainers who had eager audiences hanging on every word) that it was at Waukegan, Illinois. He grew up at Waukegan and there he went to the synagogue with his father, Meyer, an Orthodox Jewish haberdasher, who slapped him across the face with a prayer book one Yom Kippur because the boy came to services late. Later that day Kubelsky senior tried to find a way both to apologise and maintain his own dignity: "Don't you know," he asked him, "That it is a *mitzvah* to be hit with a *machzor* on Yom Kippur?"

The religious influence didn't last long with Benny Kubelsky, but we'll come to that later. For the moment we shall return to the Plaza Hotel where alone among the people in the lobby at round about midnight I recognised the ageing man – he was then about 70 – and did what comedians detest most from fans. I told him a story.

Introducing myself in the hotel elevator, I told him about the business acquaintance who had never stopped talking about the time he and Benny met at a party. The brash businessman slapped the world-renowned star on the back and said: "You can kid all you like, but *I* really *am* 39."

Benny looked at me silently and then placed his hand on his cheek, patting it painlessly although the look in his eyes was distinctly hurt. It was a kind gesture from an entertainer who had been on top since the 1920s – when he and other members of The Generation were consolidating what would soon become an international reputation.

I could have wished that the elevator floor would give way and swallow me up until I had recovered my composure. As it was, he smiled and said goodnight. Some five years later, we met again, more formally, and for a day talked about Jack Benny the man, the comedian and the Jew. We also talked once again about his being 39. It is an important part of the Jack Benny story, since he was 39 longer than anyone in recorded or unrecorded history. It became the biggest "running" gag in the story of show business, rivalled only by his own alleged meanness – which, of course, was no more true than the birth certificate he claimed to own.

He once had a fortieth birthday on the air – he was at least 60 at the time – and a combination of protests from listeners and the obvious fact that, despite all that Sophie Tucker had maintained, 39 was always a lot funnier than 40, instantly induced him to rejuvenate himself again.

On one occasion, he talked about his sister. "She used to be my younger sister Florence," he said. "Now she's my older sister Florence."

Another time he and Al Jolson were playing the perennial juveniles on a radio show. "How old are you?" Benny asked Jolie. "Thirty-eight," replied the singer. "Gee," said Jack, "we all seem to get stuck there."

Jack Benny was never a stand-up-and-joke man. In fact, he rarely told jokes at all – unless he could place himself in them. Usually he was the butt of other people's stories, a fall guy the like of which had never been seen before. He could be so taken by other people's gags that he would fall down on stage, pounding the floor. The jokes came from other comedians, such as his dearest friend George Burns – who he always said was the funniest man he knew – or from otherwise straight men such as Gary Cooper or Gregory Peck. There were times when the straight men had every gag in the show and all Benny did in the whole hour was to utter one devastating punch line. But he was happy. "Because everyone said they heard Gary Cooper or Gregory Peck on the Jack Benny show."

That showed no more conceit on his part than when Jolson dismissed his casts in the middle of a show. He simply knew not only how good he was but also what made people listen to his performances.

He was the master of the situation comedy and – as he proved that night in the elevator – of the big pause. His true genius was knowing how to mould these two characteristics into one superb performance. He employed the finest comedy writers in the world, but his special contribution was knowing how to adapt, how to edit and how to add his own touch.

He agreed that he could sometimes become involved in corny situations. "But if I am corny they have to be the greatest jokes in the world," he told me.

So what did he expect of an audience? "I expect lots of big laughs."

But although he had the reputation of being an entertainer's entertainer, and himself having a great deal of respect and admiration for, say, Bob Hope and veneration for the memory of Ed Wynn (another famous Jewish performer), he was never reluctant to criticise other show people.

"I can think of members of my club, the Hillcrest who wouldn't know good material if it hit them in the face," he said. And of Bert Lahr – yet another Jewish comic actor – he said: "He couldn't ad-lib a 'hello' ... but write him something that was good, then it was different. He was sophisticated."

So he never resented writers the way some performers did, but respected them. As he told me: "I not only respected my writers, I gave them publicity. I once said in reply to an insult: 'You'd never say that if my writers were present'."

Perhaps the finest Benny gag of all was the one in the television show in which he is accosted by a gunman. "Your money or your life," the gangster orders. For a whole minute, there is nothing but a pause – the longest minute in television history. Then the gunman repeats his demand. "Your money or your life." Once again there is silence. Finally Benny says: "Wait ... I'm thinking it over."

His real gift was in not having to think over what he did for long. He knew precisely what he could and could not do.

He knew he would never be a great violinist, although more than anything else he would have liked to be another Yehudi Menuhin or Isaac Stern. Instead, he used his love of the violin as part of his comedy act. Later, it was not his musical ability, but his respect for and adoration of professional musicians that enabled him to give concerts with the finest symphony orchestras in the world.

Irving A. Fein, Jack's manager and subsequent biographer, revealed that he raised a total of $5,901,000 in charity concerts.

His music was always Jack Benny's favourite subject.

"I'm a frustrated violinist," he told me. "It's the one thing I don't get paid for."

In the last 20 years of his life he practised every day — sometimes borrowing a violin. "But when I was a little kid I played better than I do now. I love doing the concerts now. They always review me good."

He once said: "All Jewish parents want their kids to learn violin."

His parents, in fact, even sent him to the Chicago music conservatory, but he liked that no more than he did the Waukegan High School, and left both.

However, there was no prouder moment for him than when, in the early 1970s, he was invited to visit the newly-named Jack Benny School at Waukegan. He was particularly impressed with one youngster who asked him:"Mr. Benny, how come you have the same name as our school?"

His violin playing certainly suffered when he stopped taking lessons — a point confirmed by the old teacher whom he met again for the first time when Jack was one of America's most popular TV stars. The old man didn't remember having taught Benny Kubelsky but accepted that he had. "And what do you do now, may I ask?" he said after the formal introductions.

It was not until 1956 when, quite by accident – the way he insisted the important things in his life had always happened – he started tinkering with a violin in his show. A woman asked him what he would have liked to be had he not become a comedian. He picked up a fiddle to show her and the old magic returned. Once he had established his musical frustrations, offers to play came flooding in. Benny decided to accept them when he was told it could be a good means of raising funds for the country's orchestras.

Of course, it sparked off a flood of violin jokes. "Jack Benny played Mendelssohn last night," read one review. "Mendelssohn lost."

Isaac Stern put it into his kind of perspective: "When Jack Benny walks out in tails in front of 90 great musicians, he looks like the world's greatest violinist. It's a shame he has to play."

Zubin Mehta, the conductor of the Israel Philharmonic Orchestra, reported: "When Moshe Dayan heard him play, he took the patch off his eye and put it over his ear."

But Mehta, like Stern and Nathan Milstein, were Benny's genuinely good friends. When Dean Martin honoured Jack's eightieth birthday by giving him a TV "roasting" – the sort of insults you get only when you are elderly, successful and much loved – Mehta turned up to shower Benny with scorn. "Throughout Jack's violin solo at the Hollywood Bowl," he said, "the audience were glued to their seats. That was the only way he could get them to sit down."

Jack owned that the musician could have been right. "Asking Zubin, that great conductor, to conduct for me really takes guts," he said in reply. "It's like asking Van Gogh to paint 'Merry Christmas' on the window of a department store."

He was champion of the art of self-deprecation. The young Olympic swimming athlete, Mark Spitz, tried to join in the insults at the roast. Benny said he had a swimming pool every bit as long as Spitz's. "Only when I cross a pool, I call Charlton Heston and have him part it."

In typical form, he also recalled his first meeting with the abrasive Borsht belt comedian Jack Carter. "The only thing I have in common with Jack Carter is our first names," he said. "I'll tell you how well I know Jack Carter. We met about ten years ago in a department store on an escalator. He was going up I was going down. He waved at me, I waved back — and a bottle of cologne fell out of my sleeve!"

And there was James Stewart, who remembered the time that Benny had saved his life — by giving him blood. At first, he was going to pay him $150 for the blood, but as the life-giving plasma ran through his veins he decided that Jack would really only want $100. Before long, he planned to make it $50. Finally he said he was not going to insult the great Jack Benny with money at all and decided to send a thank-you card instead.

Of such stories, outstanding performers are made. And out of legends like Benny's vault and his long-standing feud with comedian Fred Allen, he became as much a part of American life as the doughnut. Although he would have insisted on going round to the bakeries and saving the bits they had left over from the holes.

He would always come round to talking about both his music and his money. "I won't tell you how much insurance I have," said Benny, "but when I go ... the Prudential goes."

And he would neatly combine the two when talking about his favourite Stradivarius. If anyone doubted that it was a genuine Strad, he would say: "Well, it had better be genuine. If it isn't, I'm out 110 bucks."

To show just how important that violin was, he would have dozens of worthless fiddles available — so that for each performance he could screech on one of them a few bars of his signature tune, "Love in Bloom" — "What a ridiculous theme song," he told me, "I just kept playing it and it stuck" — while his regular sidekick Phil Harris would come along and snap the instrument in two. On more than one occasion, he would have to make peace with an angry member of the audience

who just *knew* that Jack owned a Strad and could not understand how a man could be as callous as that, even if he did hate
Mr. Benny so.

People on Jack Benny's shows became totally believable
characters. People such as Harris, Rochester the Negro valet
with the gravel-path voice – and the high-tenor Dennis Day.
Also very much part of every Benny routine for 40 years was
his wife Mary Livingstone – a name coined from a character
who found her way into a very early Jack Benny radio script.

Jack's parents had always had a fear of their son marrying
out of the faith. But when he met Mary Livingstone they need
not have worried. Her real name was Sadie Marks, and she
worked in a department store in Los Angeles.

He went into show business not so much against his
parents' wishes as with their resignation. They wanted him to
go into the family store – *if* he couldn't become a concert
violinist. But he didn't really take to the family environment.

He had gone to the synagogue fairly regularly, particularly
before his mother died. But although he was never a tear-away
or a "loafer" – in the popular phrase of the immigrant generation of the day – he didn't see eye to eye with the Kubelsky
clan.

At the age of 17 he teamed up with Miss Cora Salisbury,
a rather ancient vaudeville pianist, and while he could just
about make a violin string vibrate, she played on the keyboard
in an act they called "Salisbury and Benny – from Grand
Opera to Ragtime". Later, he joined a man called Lyman
Woods in "Benny and Woods" – he was playing the violin
again. But he had not yet changed his name to Jack Benny. He
called himself instead Ben K. Benny – to which he later added
the subtitle "Fiddle Funology". During World War One, he
joined the U.S. Navy and took part in a sailors' concert. That
did it.

He found then that it was easier to get across to an audience
if he could spice his act with an ad-lib or two.

He changed his name finally to Jack Benny when there
seemed to be the risk of confusion with bandleader Ben Bernie,

114

who used to say "so help me" or "Yowzir" after every announcement.

When Jack first went solo, his billing read: "A few minutes with Jack Benny. His object in life is to banish the blues."

Early on, he found that by walking on stage in an almost effeminate manner he could establish for himself a trademark that would be as identifiable as later on would be his age and his bank account.

One evening in a vaudeville show, the kind that still makes even hardened veterans quake, he walked on stage with a bright "Hello" ... to which someone in the audience countered "Goodbye". Without stopping, Jack simply walked straight into the opposite wing and out of the theatre. It has become an episode in American theatrical folklore.

He dusted off that horrific moment to form part of an early radio script as well as countless live performances later on. "This is Jack Benny ...," he announced. "There will now be a slight pause while everyone says, 'Who cares?'"

By now, it has been established that no one better understood the art of the pause than Jack Benny. One night at the London Palladium, Jack followed Phil Harris who had just received a tumultuous round of applause. As the audience kept clapping – magnified, of course, a hundred times by his own appearance – Jack simply stood on stage holding his face and waiting. But then, came an appeal from up in the "gods" in a strong cockney voice: "For God's sake", it shouted, "say something."

His audiences always took his pauses as seriously as his meanness. To dispel rumours that he really was stingy with money, Jack would go out of his way to show that he was the most generous man in show business. Once, Eddie Cantor asked him to take part in a charity benefit, but he was unable to do so. So instead, he gave Cantor a blank cheque and asked him to fill in the amount he wanted. Eddie wrote $25,000 and the sum was duly honoured.

He once gave a Los Angeles taxi driver an outrageously large tip. The cabbie turned to him and said: "Gee, Mr. Benny,

I do wish you hadn't have done that. I wanted to go home and tell my wife that I had just given a ride to Jack Benny and he really is the stingiest man I know."

George Burns used to like to take advantage of that reputation. He and Benny once went to a famous Hollywood restaurant and agreed that both would tell the proprietor: "If you let my friend pay the bill I'll never come here again." Benny said it first and Burns said thanks.

Despite the jokes about money, he told me during our long session together that for most of his life he had never taken it seriously – indeed, for years he had a bank overdraft. "I didn't know anything about money for most of my career," he said. "I maybe lost a minimum of $50 million but God knows, I'm not complaining."

"He was a darling man," George Burns recalls now. "You know with Jack Benny, only big things happened to him all the time, so he got excited about little things.

"He once signed a television contract which was worth hundreds of thousand of dollars. And I could see he was pleased with himself – as he should have been. I told him, 'Jack you're looking very happy …' and he said, 'Yes, I discovered a way of driving down Wilshire Boulevard at a steady 30 miles an hour so that you can miss every red light.'

"Or he'd say: 'Have you taken a shower at the club today?' and I'd say, 'No'. He'd say, 'Well try it, the towels are great'."

Burns was the man who could make Jack fall down on the floor prostrate, banging his hands in sheer desperation. He once suggested that Jack should stand up on a table completely naked pretending to be a standard lamp. Benny obeyed his friend to the letter … and then changed colour when the chambermaid walked in expecting to take away his room service tray

On another occasion – which became a routine they constantly practised on each other – Burns rang Jack in London and then deliberately hung up in mid-conversation.

Burns used to call him "a quiet riot."

He used to protest to Jack, who would burst out laughing

116

just by looking at him, that he wasn't doing anything funny. "I know," said Benny. "But you're doing it on purpose."

Benny was better on radio than he had been in vaudeville and sometimes better on television than he had been on radio. But always it was the pause, the slap on the cheek, the big successful guest star who took precedence over any one gag. He could be devastating with a seemingly straight line – like the time he recalled a chorus imported into Las Vegas from Paris. "There were 60 topless girls," he would say, "or were there 61 …?"

It should not be forgotten that he was also a formidable film personality. His most famous role was in a disastrous Warner Brothers flop called *The Horn Blows at Midnight* – which he would talk about self-mockingly in the same way as he talked about his other failings in life (a technique that would be copied years later by Ben Lyon in England when referring to *Hell's Angels*).

He should also be remembered for *To Be or not To Be* in which he played a Shakespearean actor in war-time Warsaw who dresses as a Nazi and gets confused with the local Gestapo chief. Some of the lines seem tasteless today – "They call me Concentration Camp Erhardt, do they?" – but the film, directed by Ernst Lubitsch, has become a classic.

In 1974 he was to have made a movie comeback as one of the two *Sunshine Boys*. But he never did. Before filming could begin, he was dead – at the age of 80.

He never told Jewish jokes as such and usually kept his Judaism to himself. Neither did he go to synagogue. "I'm not proud of it, but there it is," he told me. "I think that perhaps I might be bored and would rather go out and play golf." He didn't like golf very much either and his idea of a pleasant surprise was to wake up on the day that he had planned to spend on the links and discover it was raining.

He always gave generously to Jewish charities and, in addition to playing his violin in Israel, frequently entertained at Israel Bond rallies and on other charitable occasions.

It was at the almost totally Jewish Hillcrest Country Club

one evening soon after World War Two that he hosted the now celebrated benefit performance given by Al Jolson – the one signalling the fact that Jolson was ready for a comeback. "I'm here this evening," he said, "by virtue of the fact that Bob Hope is a gentile."

If Jewish jokes had to be told he wanted to hear them from Jews. "I have a friend, a dear man who isn't anti-Semitic or anti-anything at all," he told me, "but when he tells me Jewish jokes I have to tell him that I wish he didn't do them. They just don't sound right from a gentile."

He had very firm views about why Jews went into show business. "I think because even if they are not very good at it, they push all they can – and they know that they can always go back to selling neckties."

As for himself: "I think I'm a kind of nice Jewish fellow who doesn't want to harm anyone."

Irving Berlin
(born 1888)

Irving Berlin

The Melody Lingers On

He was born in Russia, gave himself the name of a German city and went on to write what became almost the National Anthem of America.

The son of a synagogue cantor, he produced the most successful Christmas song of all time.

And that is why Irving Berlin, song writer, takes his place among the top Jewish entertainers. True, he began as a singing waiter – after having learned to sing in the synagogue, and did on odd occasions perform on the stage – but it is as America's musical Poet Laureate that he made his name.

In all, he has written something like 3,000 songs – every one of them thumped out originally on the black notes of an old upright piano that had a gear lever to change key for him. For that was the only way he knew how. He holds what is undoubtedly the record output for any one man – yet he has never learned to read or write music. As he once told me himself: "I may have written more hits than anyone else, but I'll let you into a secret – I've written more flops, too."

One should not, however, be deluded into thinking that here is a man who can match his incredible talent with an equally amazing modesty. Berlin, then fast approaching 90, knew exactly how talented he was and how much he had contributed to the world of the popular song. More than that, he had contributed a great deal to the theatre, simply by writing its most cherished anthem: "There's No Business Like Show Business".

He could, just as easily, have called it "There's No Business Like the Music Business" – although anyone doing it for him would doubtless have heard from his lawyers the following morning. Berlin doesn't like people playing or singing his songs in any way other than the way in which he wrote them. In fact, his sheet music used to contain a warning against changing the lines. His eleventh commandment was always: "Thou shalt not parody" – a motto he adopted after achieving one of his first big successes with a little thing called "That Mesmerising Mendelssohn Tune", unquestionably a parody of the "Spring Song".

He was never just another song writer, either in the business or in the artistic sense of the term. Berlin wrote those 3,000 songs because he wanted every one of them to be a hit. In the event, half of them were never published. But he always knew what he was doing. Not only did he write most of his own music and lyrics – and after 1914 all of them – he published them, too. When his firm needed a hit, he looked in his filing cabinet and came up with a tune he had sometimes discarded years before – occasionally exactly as it was, often with a new lyric or title.

In 1917, Irving wrote a tune called "Smile and Show Your Dimple". The trouble was that nobody smiled and not a dimple was produced. So the ditty was stored away until the time came for it to be useful again. That turned out to be in 1933 – by which time Berlin felt ready for a new hit song. He called it "Easter Parade". The story continues. Three years earlier for the Al Jolson picture *Mammy*, he wrote a song called "To My Mammy". It contained the line: "How deep is the ocean ... how high is the sky?" Nobody seemed interested in providing an answer to either question – until two years later when it seemed safe to resurrect the line as the title of a tune (Berlin's own favourite word for what he produces).

He was never much of a performer, but he made his impact just as assuredly as if he had Jolson's voice and Eddie Cantor's effervescence. In his very early days he sang from the balcony of Tony Pastor's Music Hall. In 1911 after a sensational success with "Alexander's Ragtime Band" he played that song and a whole succession of other ragtime hits in theatres all over America. Two years later at a season at the London

Hippodrome, he was billed as the Ragtime King – the difficult thing was to try to convince the audience that every single ragtime number ever written was not necessarily his own work. "Other people write rags, too," he told them, but was not exactly broken-hearted when they failed to believe him.

At the end of the First World War, Irving Berlin received an invitation he couldn't refuse – from Uncle Sam. As ever, the only way to make life bearable was to turn for consolation to song writing and then to performing. He wrote an army show called *Yip Yip Yaphank* and, in his tight-fitting uniform with the Boy Scout hat, he sang from his heart: "Oh How I Hate to Get up in the Morning".

As he told me: "When I'm sad I write sad songs; when I'm in love I write love songs, and because I hated getting up early in the morning, I wrote 'Oh How I Hate to Get up in the Morning'."

I was a seven-year-old schoolboy when I heard Berlin sing that song from the stage of the London Palladium. It was in a World War Two show called *This is the Army*. I related to that number as if it had been written for me.

When he recorded it for the soundtrack of the film version *This Is the Army* an engineer was heard to say: "If the guy who wrote the song could hear the way this guy is murdering it, he'd turn over in his grave."

Berlin always had a little soft voice, "just above a whisper" as Ethel Merman says, "always sounding as though he had perennial laryngitis". Stuttering comedian Joe Frisco summed up the way Berlin sold his own songs, clutching a microphone for dear life: "You gotta ... hug him to ... hear him," he said.

Generations hugged Berlin as they heard him, without knowing who he was. Only that he had discovered the art of saying what they themselves felt. His songs were never sophisticated like Cole Porter's; rarely as imaginative as George Gershwin's or quite as romantic as Jerome Kern's. Yet it was Kern who said of him: "Irving Berlin has no place in American music. He *is* American music."

Gershwin was equally affected by the Berlin influence. He

122

once asked Irving for a job — as his musical secretary. Berlin told him he could have it — but would do better on his own. Gershwin, thinking of Berlin's output to date, took the advice, and told his teacher Charles Hambitzer: "This is American music. This is the way an American should write. This is the kind of music I want to write."

Berlin always claimed that one of his own very big influences had been George M. Cohan.

And as early as 1911, Cohan paid him a tribute at a Friars Frolic, an entertainment put on by the Friars Club — one of those occasions when show business enjoyed contemplating its own navel. "Irving Berlin," he said, "is a Jewboy who named himself after an English actor and a German city."

Hearing that, some people believed that the frequently lobbed charges of anti-Semitism against the Yankee Doodle Dandy composer were justified (although he did by all accounts have a very satisfactory and long partnership with Sam Harris). On this occasion, however, Cohan was offering nothing but praise: "Irvy writes a great song — a great song with a good lyric. It's music you don't have to dress up to listen to, but it is good music. He is a wonderful little fellow, wonderful in lots of ways. He has become famous and wealthy without wearing a lot of jewellery and falling for funny clothes. He is Uptown but he is there with the old Downtown hard shell. And with all his success, you will find his watch and his handkerchief in his pocket where they belong."

Irving Berlin himself admits that the roots of his brand of American music were in the synagogue (although it is not always as easy to recognise this as it is, for example, Jolson's singing style). "Of course I was influenced by going to *shul* with my father," was how he put it to me.

His father, like Jolson's, was a journeyman cantor — picking up whatever work he could whenever he could. Most of the time he was giving Hebrew lessons and supervising the kosher dietary laws in a slaughterhouse. His name was Moses Baline, father of eight children from a town in Siberia called Temun. It has become fashionable, even for members of his family, to pooh-pooh the idea of Jews living in Siberia before making the customary trek across Russia to the New World, but Irving is determined to stick by the story: "We were not all political prisoners, you know," he told me.

Little Israel Baline was three years old when he began that trek westwards. He remembered seeing a pogrom with houses burning all around him and being sheltered from the night air by his mother's feather bed – her proudest possession.

Years later he was to write a song called "Russian Lullaby" which in the days of the red-baiting McCarthy even he had a job justifying. He assured his critics that it was a song of yearning for the time when Russia would be free. It certainly wasn't free when he and the rest of the Baline family lived there.

Nor was America the "goldener medena" – the golden land, in his family's natural tongue Yiddish – that they expected. The Balines lived on Cherry Street on the borders of New York's Chinatown – which was far from the idyll they had imagined in the Russian penal colony. In their apartment block, children died of measles and adults suffocated during long hot summers. None of the flats had windows that would open. The only thing there was an abundance of was dirt and discontent.

On the floors of their block and in buildings around them, sweatshops fed the ever increasing demand for mass-produced clothes. Children slept on cutting room tables or in ribbon chests.

It was from this environment that young Israel Baline swore to himself he was going to escape. He was luckier than others who only dreamed of doing so. While his brothers sweated over sewing machines, Israel discovered the delights of a piano.

His father had died when the boy was eight years old and like the other children he had gone out earning a penny here, two bits there – all of which would be ceremoniously dropped into his mother's open apron each night. "I'll buy you a rocking chair out of my money one day, Ma," said young Israel.

He was truer to his word than ever he thought possible. He not only bought her a rocker, but before very long a house, too. He did it by selling papers, by singing in a saloon run by another Jew, the swarthy "Litvak" known as Nigger Mike – and by discovering that piano. It was an old upright on which the bar room pianist would bang out the hits of the day, when it was not serving as a convenient rest for the frothing glasses of beer.

There was no one around to teach young Izzy, as he liked to be called, how to play the instrument so he started picking out the notes for himself. Not well, but they seemed to make some kind of musical sense, just the same. Somehow, he found it a lot easier to make that sense on the black notes.

He didn't intend staying long at Nigger Mike's. In 1907 he was offered what seemed might just be the passport to escape. A rival saloon had become famous all over the city for an Italian song written by its piano player, Al Piantadosi. It was called "My Mauriuccia Take a Steamboat". Nigger Mike said he wanted one like it, too, to bring customers to his place.

Izzy provided the lyrics for a tune he called "Marie from Sunny Italy" and Nick Nicholson the pianist-in-residence wrote the tune. The song only made them 37½ cents each. But it was an historic event.

The printer misspelled Izzy's name on the front cover of the sheet music. Baline mysteriously became Berlin. The youngster – he was only 19 when it was copyrighted in 1907 – liked it. Soon afterwards – after he had written a string of songs that never amounted to anything and another one that did – he changed Israel to Irving. His friends of that era continued to call him Izzy.

The exception to the list of flops of 1908 and 1909 was a tune called "Dorando" about the Italian who failed to win the Olympic marathon championship because at the very last minute he was helped over the winning line.

Berlin himself admitted that he was often helped over the line too – that is if one can count his clever grasping of opportunities as being helped.

An indifferent tune called "Alexander and his Clarinet" was based on a bandleader called Alexander whom Irving had got to hear about. The song didn't do particularly well, but it inspired him to go on to write about a certain ragtime band.

Of "Alexander's Ragtime Band", a Chicago critic once commented: "If I were John D. Rockefeller or the Bank of England, I should engage the Coliseum and get a sextet including Caruso. After the sextet had sung it about ten times, we should have as a finale Sousa's Band march about the building tearing the melody to pieces with variations."

A visit to a barber's shop resulted in a team effort with another writer called George Whiting. As they were having their shoes shined, Whiting said: "My wife's gone to the country." Berlin countered, "Hoorah. Let's go to the theatre" – and realised what he had said. Instead of going to the theatre he went home and wrote a song – called "My Wife's Gone to the Country, Hurrah!"

Berlin found a wife himself, Dorothy, the sister of his theatrical friend E. Ray Goetz. He took her on honeymoon to Cuba – and discovered too late that she had caught typhoid, just another victim of an epidemic raging there at the time.

Only weeks after their return she was dead.

Other people go away and bury themselves in their grief. Berlin might have done so, too – except that Goetz suggested he write a song about it instead. The result was "When I Lost You", Berlin's first ballad and his biggest success to date. The year was 1912.

As he said, "When I'm in love ..." It took him a long time to recover from that tragedy. But he did it in the best way he knew, writing still more songs, many of which made their mark – if not then, a generation or more later. In the 1940s and '50s Phil Harris made popular a 1912 Berlin song called "Woodman, Woodman Spare that Tree" and Marilyn Monroe sang a number from a previous Berlin show called "A Man

Chases a Girl – Until She Catches Him". Meanwhile no Jewish wedding was complete without at least one rendering of "Yiddle on Your Fiddle (play for me some rag-a-time)" or even "Beck's Got a Job in a Musical Show", "Yiddisha Professor" and "Cohen Owes Me 97 Dollars" – titles that Berlin would doubtless prefer not to remember now.

At this time, *Variety* was already calling him "Berlin the hitmaker".

But some people were not particularly charitable about his output. A rumour was put around that Irving employed a "little black boy" musical genius to mass-produce his songs for him. The story took quite 50 years to die completely.

He invented a new song metre, the counter melody – when two seemingly unconnected verses with different tunes are sung simultaneously. It was half a century, until the introduction of stereo recordings, before the true effect could be appreciated, but it did well enough in those intervening 50 years. When he first used the idea in "Play a Simple Melody" in 1914 he had an instant success and one that would last seemingly for ever. Bing Crosby was proof enough of that. He sang it with the sons of his two marriages – 20 years apart. In 1950, Berlin had an almost as big success with "You're Just in Love" from his show *Call Me Madam*.

Berlin always read his newspapers – frequently with profitable results. The will of a lawyer called Charles Lounsbury published in a legal paper took his fancy and the result was a big hit for Al Jolson called "When I Leave the World Behind". Just as Lounsbery had willed it, the tune bequeathed songbirds to the blind and the moon to lovers; a theme borrowed by De Silva Brown and Henderson ten years or so later for their smash hit "The Best Things in Life Are Free".

Irving's greatest discovery, however, was not in the papers but regarding his old upright piano. He discovered that a handle could be fitted so that when he pulled it – rather like changing a car gear – he could change both the key in which he was playing and the sound of his new song. It was a 100-year-old idea that answered most of the problems of a man who could only play in F sharp – on the black notes.

He wasn't exactly a joy to listen to but the tunes sounded all right when played by someone else. Before long, he was dictating his tunes to a musical secretary – rather in the way of a business executive giving a letter to his stenographer. The piano itself kept Berlin amused even if his playing did not exactly enhance his musical reputation.

The man who worked with Berlin on the Crosby-Astaire film *Holiday Inn*, musical director Walter Scharf, went into fits of despair every time he heard Irving approach the keyboard. "He played with boxing gloves on," he told me.

But the piano, and several of its successors, did him proud. When he worked in a military camp writing *Yip, Yip Yaphank* and then *This Is the Army* the piano went with him. He called it his "Buick".

For the earlier show the Buick helped him write numbers like "Lazy", "Mandy" and "I Can Always Find a Little Sunshine in the YMCA".

He had been drafted into the Army as an ordinary soldier and was more morose in his khaki uniform than at any time since the death of Dorothy. But his General had the idea of raising $35,000 to provide a community house where friends and relatives of the enlisted men could be made comfortable on visits there. Berlin not only provided enough for that community house but another $50,000 on top of it. He also made *Yip, Yip Yaphank* a hit on Broadway – in which the men, on their final night at the Century Theatre, marched off stage, down the centre aisle and then to the pier from which they embarked for France.

The Buick, however, was not perfect. He thought a song called "God Bless America" was gilding the lily too much and put it in his filing cabinet. It was a good job he kept it there.

In 1938, he brought it out again, dusted it off and served it up to a willing American public as their answer to the Munich crisis. Within weeks of singer Kate Smith turning it into a hit, Americans stood up in concert halls whenever they heard it and took off their hats for it at baseball games.

The royalties for this – every penny the song ever earned – went to the Boy and Girl Scouts of America. He could afford to be generous. By that time he had also had hits with tunes like "A Pretty Girl Is Like a Melody" (always the excuse for an attractive lady to step out of a mirror or picture frame on stage or in a film), his own theme song "Say It With Music", "Remember", "Blue Skies", "Marie" and "Say It Isn't So".

Over the years Berlin earned himself a reputation as something of a loner. When other song writers gathered in the bars around Tin Pan Alley discussing tunes in the same way that newspapermen like to talk about their stories, Berlin would be at home, thumping out a melody with the same sort of single-minded dedication as a forger produces banknotes. Irving Caesar, one of the most successful lyricists of the century – his own hits include the words of "Swanee" and "Tea for Two" – put it succinctly enough. "Irving", he said, "was never one of the boys." It was not that he enjoyed his solitude. Sometimes, it gave rise to those moments of acute depression that seem to characterise the career of Irving Berlin. On other occasions, it just produced million-dollar triumphs such as "All Alone", "All By Myself" and "What'll I Do?"

People close to Berlin – and there have never been many of them – have said that his insomnia is his worst enemy. He turned that to good use, too – with a song called "Count Your Blessings Instead of Sheep". Once when it appeared he had taken his own advice and actually managed to sleep for a full eight hours, he came down to breakfast looking remarkably chirpy. "I see you slept last night," said a friend. "Yeh," he allowed, "But I dreamed that I didn't." When he was in a good mood, he expressed that in song, too. And when in love, he put that into his lyrics. "Always", one of his biggest hits of all, he presented to his second wife Ellin after a whirlwind courtship that captured more headlines in its time than any other items about him.

He and Ellin McKay had eloped after Ellin's multi-millionaire father, the head of the giant Postal Telegraph Company, indicated that he considered a marriage with the

Jew Berlin to be far beneath her station. A few years after their elopement in 1926, McKay was reconciled. Irving got him out of hock when he fell victim to the Wall Street Crash.

The romance became one of the most successful marriages in show business history, and the former runaways are just two years off their diamond wedding.

Fred Astaire said that Berlin "started it all" as far as modern music was concerned. Berlin is equally generous. "I would never have written 'Cheek to Cheek' or 'Top Hat, White Tie and Tails' had it not been for Fred Astaire," he says more modestly then usual.

Astaire-Rogers films like *Carefree*, *Top Hat* and *Follow the Fleet* were to add new standards to the American popular song repertoire. But "Top Hat" was just one example of the way Irving Berlin could write a song for an artist in the same way as his tailor could make him a suit.

For Astaire and Crosby he wrote "I'll Capture Her Heart — Dancing, Singing" and then a film later, "A Couple of Song and Dance Men". For Al Jolson, there was the famous "Let Me Sing and I'm Happy".

Not even Irving Berlin, however, could have predicted the success that the film *Holiday Inn* would bring him. For years he had dreamed of being able to corner the market in holiday songs. After all, for Easter he already had the famous "Parade"; "God Bless America" was always played on the fourth of July or Washington's Birthday, but Christmas presented a problem. How could you produce a tune to rival "Silent Night"?

But he did. As everyone now knows, Bing Crosby sang about his dreams of a "White Christmas" and Irving Berlin became richer than even he could have thought possible.

Even after monster successes, Berlin was never the easiest man to work with. "He'd lay down all sorts of laws and I think he'd go up the wall if anyone tried to parody his stuff," Bing Crosby told me. "But he was ever enthusiastic and somehow everyone else caught that enthusiasm. He'd make you share it.

130

He wrote what was right for his singers. I'm lucky to have had him."

During the run of *Holiday Inn*, Irving showed just how difficult he could be. There was a problem about blending a sudden change of season from winter to spring. Arranger Joe Lilley wanted a modulation of notes. "I'll tell you what we're going to do, Irving," said Lilley. "We'll get to the end of the song and on one note, one note, we'll dissolve to the next scene."

"Just so long as it's one of my notes," said Berlin.

"White Christmas" has to date sold more than 100 million records – "quite impressive," as Berlin allows. And that is him, quite impressive. But also very insecure, very anxious.

"Every time he wrote a song it was as if he were having a baby," says Walter Scharf today. There is a story that Berlin always appeared to be very haggard after writing his most successful tunes. On one occasion a rival song writer saw him looking even worse than usual. "Oh," he said, "another hit I suppose."

Holiday Inn was made at a time when Berlin still had to complete plans for another smash – *This Is the Army* which was to eclipse completely *Yip, Yip Yaphank*. It ran from 1942 to the end of 1945, playing on Broadway, in Hollywood, and then in Europe and the South Pacific. In all, it raised $9,800,000 for Service charities.

It gave Irving the chance to meet some very important people, like the Mountbattens in Britain, who obtained a special paper ration so that Irving's tribute to the "Tommy", "My British Buddy", could be published. He also met Winston Churchill.

He had been invited to have lunch at 10 Downing Street. The two men talked a little about the war in general terms and then the Prime Minister asked: "What's your view of war production in the United States?" "Oh, we're doing fine," said Irving.

"What do you think of Roosevelt's chances for re-election?"

131

"Oh," said Berlin, "I think he'll win again."

"Good," said the Prime Minister, "Good."

"But in fact, if he doesn't run again, I don't think I'll vote at all."

"You mean," said Churchill, "you mean that you think you'll have a vote?"

"Well I sincerely hope so," Irving replied.

"How wonderful," said Churchill. "How wonderful if Anglo-American co-operation ever reached the point that we could vote in each other's elections. Professor you must come to lunch some day." At which point Berlin was shown out by a smiling and grateful Prime Minister.

The great war leader had been under the impression he had been talking to Professor Isaiah Berlin.

It didn't exactly boost the confidence of a man like Irving Berlin who could only produce songs that were expected of him and who always had to have a deadline. Years later, another song writer, Sammy Cahn, put the matter into perspective. "Which came first," he was asked, "the music or the lyric?" "Neither," he replied, "the telephone call." The one that commissioned the tune in the first place, that is.

There is no better example of this than the celebrated Friday that Irving called on Messrs. Rodgers and Hammerstein to discuss his score for a show he had just taken over from the newly deceased Jerome Kern – about the Wild West heroine Annie Oakely. The show was to be called *Annie Get Your Gun*.

That night he took his wife and three daughters to their retreat in the Catskill Mountains and two days later, like Moses descending from another mountain, came down bearing two tablets – of manuscript paper. Inscribed on them were the music and lyrics for "They Say It's Wonderful" and "You Can't Get a Man With a Gun".

He still couldn't read a note of the music that his secretary had been called in to write and he still punched the keyboard of his F sharp piano. But a matter of weeks later he had numbers like "Anything You Can Do, I Can Do Better",

"The Girl that I Marry", "My Defences Are Down", "Doin'
What Comes Naturally", "I Got the Sun in the Morning" and
"Lost in His Arms".

Ask Irving Berlin what his own favourite songs are and the
answer comes easily: "The ones that were the biggest hits." He
had reason to like *Annie Get Your Gun* a great deal. It set an
all-time record. Almost every song from the show turned out
to be a hit.

The most notable of these was the result of a last-minute
request from Oscar Hammerstein to produce a number suit-
able for a stage-wait, the part of the show when a particularly
difficult set is being prepared behind the curtain and the artists
have to perform in front of a backcloth.

Hammerstein thought Irving had just the right number, but
he couldn't see it among the mass of papers produced for their
story conference. "I left it out," said Berlin.

"In heaven's name, why?" asked the great lyricist-turned-
impresario.

"I didn't think you liked it," Irving answered. "You didn't
say enough."

That number was a little thing called "There's No Business
Like Show Business". As Hammerstein said: "He was just
going to throw it away. Now, out of context of the play, it's
merely the song that *means* show business."

Hammerstein quipped at the time: "Irving has no sophisti-
cation about it. He just loves hits."

As he himself readily admits with these quick jabs about
writing more flops than anyone else, he didn't always succeed.
He did a show called *Miss Liberty* which never really took off,
and in 1962 had the biggest flop of his career, a show based on
the love affair that the American people were having at the
time with the Kennedys. It was called *Mister President*. Since
then he has done very little – but paint.

In between the two flops, however, there had been a show
called *Call Me Madam*, a then topical piece about a woman
ambassador to a mythical grand duchy (at about that time,
Perle Mesta was appointed American envoy to Luxembourg).

133

That, too, was brimful with hits, "It's a Lovely Day Today", "The Hostess With the Mostest", "Marrying For Love", and that counter-melody piece called "You're Just in Love".

That number, too, had been an afterthought. The producers thought that a big piece was needed for the second act. Irving went away to New Haven, Connecticut, for a night and came back with "You're Just in Love" the following morning. As his star Ethel Merman recalled: "We didn't have it Saturday. Monday morning we had a hit."

Dwight D. Eisenhower had a hit from the show, too – in a comedy routine speculating on the possibility of his running for the presidency. Irving conjured up a jokey number called "They Like Ike". It not only became the Republican Party's theme song at the conventions but also the slogan for Eisenhower's entire campaign, changed only slightly to "I Like Ike".

Ike showed his appreciation. At the President's suggestion, Congress voted $1,500 to the cost of striking a special medal for Mr. Berlin. Eisenhower presented it to him and read out the citation: "In recognition of his services in composing many popular songs including 'God Bless America'."

As I said, he has usually looked a lot more modest than he really is – and not just about his music. At his favourite restaurant, he always liked the head waiter to go through the menu with him. One evening, the recommendation turned out to be superb, but Irving was going out of town and he wanted the maitre d'hôtel to know that his absence from the restaurant would not be for any other reason.

"Very good, sir," said the man in the tail coat. "If any of your friends can't read either, I'll be happy to help them, too."

He had very definite views on modern song writers – much of whose work he can't understand. In the early 1970s he picked out two contemporary songs that he *did* like, "The Impossible Dream" and "Little Green Applies". But he was sure that neither had been produced by professional songsmiths.

"A professional song writer would never have rhymed 'little

134

green apples' with 'and it don't snow in Minneapolis','' he told me.

"Shall I tell you what I would have said?" As if I could have stopped him. "God didn't make little green apples and we don't pray in churches and chapels." A new Irving Berlin lyric for free!

As for his own songs, he likes them better now than when he first wrote them. "My songs sound better – and they pay more, too. Royalties and recording fees have gone up."

He has always kept firm tabs on the music business. Back in the '30s he thought he detected an undesirable trend: "They've made song hits into background music. Songs that were hits before radio are still hits. Songs that were made hits by radio and films are forgotten."

This is not strictly speaking true. Films engraved his songs on people's memories and radio and recordings helped to establish them permanently to form part of their lives.

But he is not so sure he likes being called an "institution". As he explained: "You know the old gag – who the hell wants to live with an institution?

"Let's use the word 'success', I like that better. Some people think I work too hard, but the important thing for me is to keep going." But he doesn't like the big "tzimmis" people make about his age. He may have married a society bride and become an institution, but the old Yiddish words still slip easily from his tongue.

He will still talk about his songs with friends – but only on the phone. He doesn't like making personal appearances even in private. Even now, he still refuses to be "one of the boys" – and there are few of them left. When, recently, most of America's leading composers were asked to provide material for a hall of fame being established in New York, Berlin made it plain that he would rather not.

One thing cannot be denied. He has always been the sort of man to put things into what he regards as their true perspective. When he bought a house in Beekman Place, one of New York's most fashionable areas near the East River, he said

135

"I've always lived near this river, ever since I came to New York. It's a more swanky neighbourhood maybe, but the same tugboats pass by."

On the days when he is depressed and looking for solace, his painting is more important than ever.

One of his small grand-daughters once boasted about her famous grandfather, Irving Berlin. "What does he do?" she was asked. "Oh," she replied, "he paints."

He specialises in birds. When he found that one of them looked better wearing a top hat, he added a cane too – and sent it off to his friend Fred Astaire. He then followed it with several others in the same genre – all of which have pride of place on Astaire's den walls.

But all of them have one particular characteristic – none have hands or feet. Astaire wanted to know why. "I can't paint hands or feet," Irving replied. As he says himself: "As a painter I'm a pretty good song writer." As a song writer, he's a pretty good song writer, too. And he always has been.

"I've always thought of myself as a song writer," he says. "Do you want big words like composers? I won't be modest. But I'm a song writer like dozens of others. And as long as I'm able, whether the songs are good or bad, I'll continue to write them because song writing is not just a business with me. It's everything."

In 1983, Tin Pan Alley paid tribute to him. The songwriters of New York gave him a party to mark his ninety-fifth birthday. He didn't turn up, but spoke to the organisers on the phone.

He wrote his epitaph with his tune, "The Song Is Ended". His songs have not ended. To misquote the same number, their melodies linger on.

George Burns
(born 1896)

George Burns

Sunshine Boy

In the days when television sets were big and square and their screens small and rounded, few programmes were more popular than the one centred around the dumb blonde and her husband who didn't seem to have to do much more than point with his big cigar.

George Burns would ask his wife Gracie Allen why she put salt in the pepper pot and she would explain: "Everyone keeps mixing them up, pouring pepper when they want salt. This way, when they make a mistake, they'll be right."

It was, said George Burns, perfectly logical. "Or what we used to call illogically logical. It was the sort of thing that made sense only to Gracie."

For a couple who were as much in love as they were, the most illogical thing she ever did, so far as he is concerned, was to die of a sudden heart attack. But George Burns didn't allow his sense of humour to die with her. At the age of 89, with his very first Oscar perching on the mantelpiece of his home in Beverly Hills, George Burns remains one of the funniest men in America.

He too started life as the son of a synagogue cantor – as Nathan Birnbaum in 1896 – and that alone would have qualified him for membership of The Generation. "My father had what we call a disappointment act. You know what that is? Well, when another cantor got sick, my father went out and took his place. He wasn't a very good cantor."

In those days he himself was one of a large family on the East Side of New York who lived much as other Jewish families of the neighbourhood and of the age – from hand to mouth.

It was a postman – "a letter carrier" as the Americans called him – who first gave him the idea of trying his hand at show business. He was about seven at the time, and has been trying it ever since.

If Burns himself can be believed he did so with varying degrees of success. Most of the time according to him succeeding only in being a very good failure – except that he became a brilliant performer just before it was too late.

As a small child, he joined the Peewee Quartet who sang whenever they could get a crowd to hear them. "I used to watch a buck dancer in the Hamilton Fish Park. I learnt to dance and I learnt how to pass the hat around when they gave you pennies. I also learnt how if they gave you a dime, to hide it from the rest of the kids.

"We used to sing on ferry boats. If they liked you, they'd give you coins. If they didn't, they'd throw you overboard. It got so I could only sing when I had water in my mouth."

At the age of seven he decided to become a Presbyterian. The Peewee Quartet had got a job singing at the local Presbyterian church and each member of the group had been given a 70-cent watch. "I told my mother I didn't want to be Jewish any more. I had been Jewish for seven years and hadn't made a penny. I was a Presbyterian for a day and already I had a watch. My mother said, 'Help me hang out the wash. Then you can become a Presbyterian.' Well, I did and some water got in the watch – and it stopped. So I decided to become Jewish again."

About this time, he decided he would do better if he looked older. He found a pair of pince-nez lying on the ground and took to wearing them because he thought they added a mature look to his appearance. "They belonged to a man of about 70. I used to think that a man of 70 was very old. Now if I meet a man of 70, I send him out for a glass of water."

Strangely enough, the octogenarian who is one of its last survivors was one of the babies of the pack.

He began to get jobs singing and then dancing, too, on the vaudeville stage – always in small time, avoiding the lucky break as others tried to avoid the boom and the hook on amateur nights. If he thought about jokes, they came usually from two different sources – both of them comic magazines. One was called *College Humor*, the other *Whiz Bang*. "My idea of twisting a joke was taking one out of *College Humor* and saying it came from *Whiz Bang*," he says in his own very special self-deprecating way. The real showman in him is revealed in the way he has learned to regard every conversation as a performance, every word in an interview and – if his friends can be believed – in normal day-to-day chat as if it were part of a carefully honed script.

Burns had had many guises on the stage. He once called himself Willy Dwight. Before a chorus girl friend introduced him to the Irish Catholic Gracie Allen, he teamed up with another partner and did a roller-skating act which they first called Brown and Williams. When that didn't work particularly well, they changed it to Williams and Brown. That wasn't much good either. So they tried Brown and Brown and then Williams and Williams.

For a while, he maintains, every kid on the East Side was called either Brown or Williams. "Kids growing up there thought they were gentiles. We'd be booked for one-nighters, five dollars and car fare."

Eventually, he was to do better as half of Burns and Allen.

Sometimes, they even managed to get the managements to applaud as they danced – "I was always a left footed dancer; my right foot was usually laying off."

He once did an act with a performing seal – deputising for a certain Captain Betts who went everywhere with his seal Flipper. "The captain got sick and he asked me if I'd go down to the 14th Street Theatre and play with the seal. I said I didn't think I could do it, but he told me not to worry. 'The seal,' he said, 'is the whole act. You throw him a ball and he bounces it on his nose. Then you give him a piece of fish. He plays Yankee

140

Doodle on the pipes and the American flag pops up. You just throw him another fish.' "

The trouble was that his pockets were always full of fish. And if you still believe him – and the story is as much a part of American show-biz legend as was the success of Burns and Allen years later – he had a date that night with a girl with the improbable name of Trixie Levene.

Trixie wasn't put off. "She never noticed the smell because she was working with Fink's Mules. In fact, she congratulated me on my after-shave lotion."

It was just one of the many things he did, making a crust here and there because, he insists, he just loved show business.

"I danced a Russian mazurka once in a Spanish costume because I didn't know the difference.

"I did a roller dog act in Romkoncoma and there isn't much lower than that – especially as I knew nothing about dogs. I just heard there was a vacancy, picked up a couple of stray dogs in the street and told them I had a dog act."

It was, in fact, 27 years before George Burns began to hear the kind of applause that comes only to a big star. In those years if he saw great performers like Jolson entertain, he did so from the gallery – for that was all he could afford.

"I stayed working for 27 years because I loved it. I was bad in those days – but I didn't know I was bad because the theatres were worse than I was."

One thing Burns proved beyond all doubt was that he had staying power.

"For a comedian to last," he says, "it is important to know what to do off the stage as well as on – because if you get material that's no good, you have to recognise it."

More important, the audience has stayed with him.

"I'll tell you when audiences change. If you've laid off for ten years and then come back – then you'll find the audience has changed, because they will have forgotten you. But if you don't go away, they'll think they're seeing something new all the time. You won't even grow old that way."

It should not be forgotten that this little man, who now wears thick-lensed spectacles and talks with a raspy voice so that you feel you should go out and get him a glass of water, was also a businessman.

He not only owned the rights to the Burns and Allen show first on radio and then on television, but to three or four other shows, too. "I kept going from one room to the other to find out what was going on," he told me.

His act with Gracie, once they had decided to leave the dogs, seals and dancing behind them, was exceedingly simple. "I'd ask her how her brother was and for the next 45 minutes she'd tell me. All I had to do was to point my cigar. I got so good I could point with my left hand or my right."

Gracie was not always the easiest person to work with. He would feed her a line and if she didn't like it, would answer with complete silence.

"I could have silence for a week. Finally, she said a line one night and it got a laugh so she said it all the time.

"Once in the middle of our act I asked her a question and instead of answering it she said: 'Ladies, don't send your clothes to the Strathmore Cleaners. I sent them a perfectly beautiful $400 dress and they ruined it, absolutely ruined it.'"

He and Gracie were together on stage and off for 38 years. "You couldn't argue with Gracie. I'd feed her straight lines like 'What are you doin' today?' And she'd say, 'I can't see you today, I'm expecting a headache.'"

Or he would say: "A funny thing happened to my mother in Buffalo," and she would say: "I thought you were born in Cleveland."

He says that the reason their marriage was so successful was that he didn't take his work home with him. "I never played the big lover on the stage," he explained.

"In fact, I wasn't the world's greatest lover. When I kissed her, she never applauded.

"I find that all comedians are married for a long time simply because they are not lovers.

"We were never equal partners. I realised I couldn't do what

142

she could do on stage. So I was her straight man. I did my real work behind the scenes, organising the act, writing the material."

When Gracie retired, Burns really came into his own, in cabaret at Las Vegas and in individual appearances on TV. "*I didn't need to retire. I was retired when I worked with Gracie.*"

He says he loves show business – "Because in what other business can you walk around wearing the same colour lipstick as Dolores Del Rio?"

The thing that has endeared him to his audiences is that he isn't dirty. "There's a hole in the wall between the ladies' dressing room and mine," he said during his London show in 1975. "I've been meaning to plug it up. But what the hell ... let 'em enjoy themselves."

As he explained: "That's about as dirty as I get. I guess I'm a prude at heart. Even if I'm home alone, I close the door when I go to the bathroom."

The differences in his and Gracie's religion had no effect on their marriage. "My children were raised as Catholics," he says. "I was the only one who wore a hat on Friday nights."

Burns has a story for every occasion. He used to enjoy telling how fortunate Judy Garland was to have been discovered by Louis B. Mayer when she was ten years old.

"That could never happen to me," he said. "When I was ten years old, Louis B. Mayer was ten years old."

He likes making jokes about being Jewish in the same way as he knocks his tremendous success and revels in gagging about his age.

At home in California, he says he has two small cats. "The cats like me – of course, they don't know I'm Jewish."

But he does not particularly agree with those theories about the Jewish success in show business. "I don't think they're better than anyone else. Look at John, what's his name, the Irishman ... John McCormack. He had a pretty good act, didn't he?"

For years right from the time he started succeeding in entertainment – which was a lot longer ago than he allows – he helped support first his parents and then his brothers and sisters. He always likes talking about his sister Goldie. He claims she bought the only copy of a recent LP he made. "She played it once and then made me give her the money back."

He mingles her name in the midst of discussions about members of his "crowd" like Al Jolson and Maurice Chevalier. "I once told Chevalier: 'Maurice, would you do a favour for my sister Goldie?' He took out a picture of himself and then his fountain pen. 'No, put that away,' I told him. 'I want you to have an affair with her.' "

His greatest success has always been at telling how unimportant he is. There was, for instance, the woman he met in an hotel lift. "Just as we got to the ground floor she said: 'It's so exciting being in an elevator with a celebrity.'

'It sure is,' I replied. 'But who the hell *are* you.' "

Since Gracie's death, he has been seen frequently in the company of pretty girls. He is not concerned with sexual performance, however. "At my age, I'm lucky to have a pulse!" The clever thing about him is that he has always learned to keep his finger on the pulse of the public's taste.

At least, he has since he gave up dancing and started concentrating on telling jokes and pointing that cigar. It was George Jessel who takes credit for this switch. He couldn't understand how Burns could just be an also-ran performer on stage but the life-and-soul of all those theatrical parties. He suggested that George do on stage what he was so good at doing in private – or rather in front of his friends.

The only time he stopped using the cigar in public was in the film that earned him his Oscar – the 1975 smash *The Sunshine Boys* by Neil Simon, which tells the story of a couple of geriatric vaudevillians who worked with each other for 43 years and hated every moment of it. "I don't really think you could work with someone for 43 years and hate him," he said pensively. "It's like living with a wife whom you hate for 43 years. You couldn't do that. Or perhaps you could," he said, still puffing, still chuckling.

The 38 years he had with Gracie Allen were undoubtedly his happiest. As for show business, "I was a Sunshine Boy all my life in vaudeville." He was given the film part after the death of another Sunshine Boy – his best friend Jack Benny. "I didn't want to get the part that way, but I've got nothing to do with the feller upstairs. He handles it. He's bigger than Irving Fein."

Irving Fein was Jack Benny's agent and who, since his death, has represented Burns. He it was who got him a reading for the part.

The role was a triumph for George. But he insists he was always a film star. He made his last film *Honolulu* in 1939. "They must have liked it because they asked me back to do this one."

His part was a natural piece of acting – in which he spoke slowly, deliberately, yet still managing to reel off Simon's lines as though he had just made them up between cigar puffs.

Only it was Matthau who smoked in the film. He wasn't allowed to.

"Every time he started to smoke I'd get very close to him. Sometimes, he thought I'd got too close, so I'd tell him, 'Walter, it's the cigar I like – not you.'"

If you didn't know that the two men got on so well together

off-stage, the older Burns telling a succession of vaudeville stories to Matthau, you would not find it difficult to believe that they really did hate each other's guts.

"Acting is simple," he maintains. "You knock on the door. A guy says, 'Open the door, come in.' If you come in, you're a good actor."

By this time it can be seen Burns really had made it to the top – the real top. In *Oh God* in 1978 he played ... the title part. He followed it with a handful of other roles in which he really played himself – a little funny old Jewish gentleman.

On the cabaret stage and TV he was funnier than ever.

Writers make a lot of the tidiness of George Burns – tidy in his work and tidy in his appearance. He wears an immaculately styled grey wig. "I've got all sorts of hair – I've got black hair and blue hair. I've got a trunk that I part in the middle."

He says that the only domestic crisis that worries him now is if the soup is cold. "If the soup is hot, I've got no problems!"

His biggest problem of all is not having Gracie around him now. When he is in California, he goes to her grave at Forest Lawns Cemetery every day. When he is away, he saves up his news and tells it all to her at the graveside on his return. "I don't know if she can hear – wherever she is."

But, he says, he is a patient man. "I'll be seeing her soon. And I'll be taking my music along with me – in case they've got vaudeville up there."

146

Fanny Brice
(1891–1951)

Fanny Brice

Second-Hand Rose

She was the original Second-Hand Rose, but there was nothing second-hand about the way she dominated audiences on Broadway. She did it all her own way.

A new generation have come to know a name their parents barely remembered – thanks to the double screen portrayal by Barbra Streisand. But few of them have heard the actual voice of Fanny Brice, fewer still would recognise a photograph of her. Hers was not the sort of act or voice that in its original form could cross the time barrier. But no history of show business could afford to overlook her. In her time she ranked with Jolson, Cantor and Tucker. She was not just *of* The Generation, she was one of its corner stones.

She was talented, so she exploited every ounce of that talent. She was ugly, so she exploited that, too. When the exquisite Ziegfeld girls languidly decorated the Follies' stage and with their thrust-out, partly exposed breasts made the men out front mop their brows, Fanny Brice came on to prove that if a pretty girl was like a melody an ugly girl with a big nose could be a very funny tune.

If her life had been all funny – had she been nothing but a funny girl and then a funny lady – she might have been much happier. As things were she was like the clown, crying under her make-up. And nearly all those tears were on account of the men who entered her life (for varying lengths of time). Some of them never really went out of it. Her first marriage was at the age of 15 – to a barber. It didn't last for more than a year or so. At the time, she tended to put it all down to experience – and to being just one more thing that happened to a girl born the wrong side of the Brooklyn Bridge.

148

There, synagogues sprouted as regularly as the trashcans. But she was not particularly religious although she never forgot (or was allowed to forget) her Brooklyn roots.

Nor did she ever forget she was Jewish. Forget? On the surface her Jewishness may not have gone much further than a taste for chopped liver and an accent that was as commercial as a circus march.

Her father was a loving man – a saloon keeper his regulars knew as Pinnochle Charlie. Her mother was Hungarian – and very much the boss of the family. Years later, when Fanny was entertaining Presidents, Mama was the one who had to be introduced first.

Fanny had sung her first song when she was 13 in 1904. Her name was Fanny Borach then. The tune she sang was to prove to be a fair indication of her intended philosophy in life: "When You Know You're Not Forgotten by the Girl You Can't Forget".

She was full of punch, oozing not with sex appeal but with chutzpah – and in an age when girls dared no more to speak up for themselves than they contemplated showing a shapely ankle, that was almost the same thing.

Very early on, she found a place in the chorus of a George M. Cohan show – and just as quickly left. Cohan, the man who was almost never seen on stage without an American flag trailing behind him, didn't like her. But other people in show business, every bit as important, did.

In 1910 she sang the eighth song (there were to be something like 2,992 more) written by a young composer named Irving Berlin. It was called "Sadie Salome Go Home". She and the song were big hits.

Berlin liked her and she liked his song. She was to say about it: "That Berlin song summed up Lischa on the Coney Island popcorn counter and Marta of the cheeses at Brodsky's Delicatessen and all the Sadies and the Rachels and Birdies with the turn-over heels at the Second Avenue dance halls."

She sang it in a show called *The College Girls*. It was burlesque – but she was not on the burlesque wheel or the "old

149

burlecue", as the regulars called it, for long. A man who was very much his own talent scout heard about the outrageous, gawky girl with the big nose and loud voice and took himself along to a performance. As a result he offered her a job. His name: Florenz Ziegfeld Junior. The job: comedienne to the Follies.

"How much do you want?" he asked her. Young Fanny – by this time Borach had become Brice – took a deep breath and stammered without being able to avoid making it sound like a question: "$40?" He said he thought he could go to $75 – providing she guaranteed him a year's work. It was like matzo crumbs from heaven.

Ziegfeld took to Fanny as he did to few other of his performers, although he never developed the same romantic attachment for her as he did later for stars such as Anna Held, Billie Burke or Marilyn Miller.

Ziegfeld gave her a new song to sing – "Lovie Joe" – although it wasn't liked by Abe Erlanger, one of the organisers of the famous Broadway "Syndicate" who decided which shows played at which theatre and even told Ziggy what to do. Only the young, untried Fanny Brice dared tell him that she didn't care what he thought.

"I live on 128th Street," she said. "It's on the edge of Harlem. They all talk that way."

Erlanger was ready for a fight. "You're out," he screamed. "No one says 'No' to me on the stage." So she left.

It took an SOS from Ziegfeld, in the form of one of his famous telegrams sent to her boarding house, to bring her back – and to give her the chance to make her Ziegfeld debut in the Atlantic City try-out.

However back in New York again the song had to be dropped. Erlanger had spoken. Fanny's answer was to squeeze herself into a too-small dress, put on a black-face make-up and pull her skirt up to her bloomers. The house collapsed. As she danced into the wings – or perhaps hobbled is a better description – Erlanger handed her a straw hat. A hat with the crown pulling away from the brim.

He said he had broken it applauding her – from then on the boater never left her possession. On another occasion, the great beauty Lilliane Lorraine had a fist fight with Fanny in the wings – in which they clawed at each other and even ripped their gowns. The fight ended with Fanny dragging the kicking Lorraine out into the centre of the stage while the audience applauded ecstatically.

Despite her ungainly appearances, Fanny did have the men running after her, and she always seemed to be in love. But her real love was reserved for a professional gambler and small-time gangster – a role never hinted at in *Funny Girl* – called Nick Arnstein.

He could do whatever he liked with her, treat her as badly as he saw fit.

Arnstein liked to call himself Nick Arnold – perhaps he didn't like showing that some of the biggest crooks as well as the greatest show people of his age were Jews.

He didn't look particularly Jewish. In fact, he was tall, handsome and – as George Jessel has described him in his book *Elegy in Manhattan* – "with the manners of an English earl".

Above all, he was a con man, playing cards on boats in the old Mississippi tradition. But it was rumoured that even the stewards and cabin boys could beat him at a game of poker.

When Arnstein got involved in a $5 million robbery, Fanny helped him in every way she could. She even borrowed $240,000 from Ziegfeld in an attempt to get Arnstein out of trouble. But it didn't. He did a stretch in Sing Sing, always protesting that he was innocent – Fanny protesting with him along the way.

Arnstein was said to have masterminded the crime. "Mastermind?" she screamed. "Mastermind? He couldn't mastermind an electric light bulb into the socket."

In short, he was not really very clever. Fanny found the best way of defending his innocence was to show exactly how inept he was. "If Nicky ever went out to steal anything," she told Jessel, "he would have come back empty-handed and somebody would have copped his watch."

But although she divorced Arnstein, she couldn't get him out of her mind. She prided herself on always being able to spot a phoney, but didn't apply the rule to him.

He gave her two children, Frances and Bill. When she left a Follies show cast to have one of the babies, Ziegfeld sent an angry telegram complaining about her lack of consideration.

In every show, she had the audience falling out of their seats and rolling in the aisles with her Jewish dialect routines – one, about a trip to Coney Island, was particularly memorable. But unlike Barbra Streisand, she knew when to leave the chopped-liver voice behind, and away from the stage she usually did.

And sometimes she did in public too – never more effectively than when she stood on stage, propping up a lamp post, her face covered in dust and sang the plaintive "My Man", a song that had been brought over from France – as "Mon Homme" – by Mistinguett. Ziegfeld didn't like the French chanteuse and sent her back on the next ship. Fanny was chosen to sing the number in her place. For the occasion, she turned up at the theatre in a red wig and shawl. Ziegfeld was so outraged that he tore them both off and smeared her face with the dust from the stage. She appeared like that night after night and "My Man" became her theme song. And every single time she sang, the audience wept.

Later, *her* man would be Billy Rose, sometime song writer, shorthand writer and superstar showman. That romance, too, was to be overdone. In truth, she once (after their divorce) pointed to his room in an apartment building and said: "Up there sits the most evil man I know."

The girl who became the epitome of the Jewish comedienne ended her days as a top radio star – playing a very unJewish four-year-old girl known to millions of American devotees as Baby Snooks.

She also became an interior decorator of note. She once said: "If I tried, I got everything in my life I ever wanted. But with men, the harder I tried, the harder I flopped."

Fanny Brice died in 1951.

Topol
(born 1935)

Topol

Who Became a Rich Man

There's a small band of entertainers who are sufficiently well known to be instantly recognised by a single name. Jolson was undoubtedly one. Crosby another. It is necessary only to bill Ella Fitzgerald as Ella.

Chaim Topol, perhaps using a particularly Israeli form of chutzpah, decided to give his audiences no opportunity for second guessing him. In the tradition of Grock and Grimaldi – although he has probably never seen himself as a clown – he decided that if he were going to be known at all it would be simply as Topol. (Which considering the problems non-Jewish audiences and critics would have with a name like Chaim – it means "life" in Hebrew – is probably quite fortunate.)

It wasn't a bad idea. The name caught on – and Topol has achieved pretty well all the success, and more so, he could have imagined.

I say pretty well, because the phenomenal success he has achieved has basically come through a single role. He has starred in *The Caucasian Chalk Circle* at the prestigious Chichester Festival in Britain, he has taken *The Baker's Wife* on tour from one end of America to the other, he has appeared in James Bond films, but it is as Tevya in *Fiddler on the Roof* that he will always be remembered – and by enough people to make him a top, if not a super, star.

Topol had seen *Fiddler* on Broadway in 1966 (the year before he opened in it in London) played by Zero Mostel – and hated every minute of it. It was a matinée performance, and he resented the way he thought Mostel patronised his audience. Mostel would go to the footlights, look out at the people in the front stalls and say things like: "You're yawning, Mrs. Finklestein. What's the matter? Your husband keep you awake last night? Am I putting you to sleep?"

It seemed, as he told me, to symbolise all the things that Israelis like himself wanted to avoid. It was a diaspora Jewish story for and by people with a diaspora outlook. *Fiddler*, after all, was based on the Sholem Aleichem tale of the milkman who struggled with the joint problems of having five daughters to be married off and trying to keep them away from the next pogrom. It surfaced in New York not so very long after young Israelis had decided that they despised everything to do with this "galut (exile) mentality". The Yiddish language and all that it stood for represented a cowering Jew – not someone of this new breed at all.

Topol was invited by his Israeli producers to play Tevya in Tel Aviv. He said no thank you – and was less than polite in his refusal.

Fiddler was, however, a tremendous smash in Tel Aviv. Topol didn't worry much about that, although doubtless the success had some bearing on what followed. There was a phone call from London: Would Topol care to audition for the show when it opened at Her Majesty's Theatre?

What had induced the London management to call on him was an Israeli film called *Sallah*. As Topol has since told me, it was virtually the same part – an elderly, bearded man with several daughters. The difference was that Sallah was a Sephardi immigrant living in Israel, whereas Tevya was steeped in the European ghetto of Anatevka (for which you could read any other shtetl within the Pale of Settlement).

Topol was 31 years old at the time. When the athletic-looking, clean-shaven Israeli actor arrived at Her Majesty's for that audition, it wasn't easy to convince the management that it wasn't some sort of hoax. He wasn't what they were expecting at all – until, that is, they heard him sing "If I Were a Rich Man".

A few months later, his rendering of that song, throwing his arms from side to side as he contemplated a future that looked all black, brought the house down.

For a year, he played the part in London and the role and London were his. Chaim saw Mostel in another evening performance in New York, and this time thought the actor brilliant. However, three years later, it was Topol, not Zero Mostel who was invited to star in the United Artists' film version. It was a masterly move, the film won universal acclaim and wrung hearts all over the world.

But it provided something of a problem for its star. "Everywhere I went, people said to me, 'When are you going to play the Topol part again.' I took it as a compliment because I think I knew what they meant."

What it did mean was that he was now typecast.

But as he told me: "If I'm going to have any difficulties at all, that's a pretty nice one to have."

In 1982, London audiences heard him wishing he was a rich man once more. He was one of the stars in a Royal Variety Show in which he relived his *Fiddler* triumph once more. The following morning, he was swamped with offers from managements wanting to put the show on again. He accepted one of them – for a limited season in the British capital for the summer of 1983. For the first time he was now old enough not

156

to need to dye the beard he was growing specially for the part. It was naturally grey.

It was certainly a good public relations exercise for the Jewish people at a time when Israel in particular was getting plenty of "stick" from the media. For unlike other Jewish entertainers, Topol has always had a particularly distinctive ingredient in his makeup. Jews liked to feel that he played a Jew who *felt* like a Jew. He is an almost fanatically proud Israeli, as involved in his country's politics as show people in Britain are in local football teams or Americans in golf.

His parents came from Europe – indeed, he says his father was a Tevya who was in turn the son of a Tevya who was himself a Tevya coming from a place very much like Anatevka.

He came from Tel Aviv, lived on a kibbutz and then worked as a printer on the daily newspaper, *Davar*, organ of the trades union organisation, the Histadrut.

What made him an entertainer was joining the Army, which is not usually considered an entertaining experience, particularly in Israel where more of its soldiers have fought in wars than those of any other country in the world.

He was assigned to a *nahal* group – a body of soldier farmers. His group also formed an entertainment outfit, and it was there that he learned his craft – singing, satirising, and making life a little easier for the men in uniform.

He started as a *nochslepper* – doing a wide variety of odd jobs behind the scenes. But it wasn't long before he was the obvious star of the outfit. Released from the Service, he joined professional theatre companies in Haifa and Tel Aviv.

He made low-budget Israeli films. He made cheaply-manufactured Hebrew records (some of which are now considered collectors' items) and finally he was offered the part in *Sallah* which led to ...

Topol will always be known as Topol, if not Tevya. But then really it is the same thing. *Topol by Topol*, the one-man show he has been preparing for years, will have much of Tevya in it.

He has other interests – including a vast ambitious scheme

for producing a filmed educational version of the Bible. Every single book of the Old and New Testament – with Chaim himself appearing only in the Old – will by the end of the century be made on video and film.

And from there? "Be healthy and strong," says Topol as he escorts all visitors to the door of either his London or Tel Aviv homes. I know what he means.

Sammy Cahn
(born 1913)

Sammy Cahn

Rhythm Is His Business

It was Sammy Cahn who described the rise of Jews in the world of show business as a climb up the "ethnic ladder". Cahn himself has leapt up that ladder across miles of sheet music – mostly furnishing lyrics in bursts of inspiration. An inspiration matched only by his powers of conversation. If this book dwelt on the top Jewish talkers, he would have to have a place in it; he can spice almost any dissertation on any event in contemporary history with an anecdote. He finds his way here because most recently, and really quite suddenly, he has become a top performer – combining his ability to talk at the drop of a microphone cable with his incredible repertoire, to the delight of audiences in London and New York.

But back to the ethnic ladder according to Mr. Cahn. "The first popular songs that gained prominence in America were written by Irishmen. And then they branched out into every other field – boxers, politicians, gangsters. All Irish-Americans.

"Then along came the Jewish immigrants and again, it started to be the Jewish politicians, the Jewish songwriters, the Jewish entertainers and, yes, we have to face it, the Jewish gangsters. They were incredibly ambitious and industrious.

"If you remember how it went, the Irish tenors and the Irish vaudevillians were suddenly replaced by Jewish singers and Jewish all-round entertainers. Then they were followed by the Italians and then by the blacks."

But even Cahn will admit that name for name, as far as the entertainment field is concerned, the Jews seem to have taken the *kichel*.

"It was," he told me in the first of perhaps a dozen conversa-

160

tions we have had since, "the simple desire to rise above your station."

Perhaps that was why they needed an ethnic ladder.

The station to which Sammy Cahn was born in 1913 was a little restaurant in New York called Cohen's. His father, Abraham Cohen, was as soft as the gefilte fish he sold. Sammy – he came after his sister Sadye and before Pearl, Florence and Evelyn – used to be able to twist Mr. Cohen around his violin finger. If he needed money, he would either raid his father's "magic box", an old tea chest in which the restaurateur kept $20 bills, or tell him that his glasses were broken. He had found a way of taking out the lens so that he could put it back again once the money for a new piece of glass was in his possession. He broke about as many pairs of spectacles as he made visits to the movies.

His mother, on the other hand, was strong and clever. She ran the household as if it were Tammany Hall, and since she was a power in the local Democratic Party, the simile is not altogether inappropriate. But she, too, had her soft spots and Sammy knew how to find them. Usually, he did so at the piano keyboard.

"Zing mir a por lieder," she would instruct in her heavy Polish-Jewish accent and he would do his best. The tunes had come out of the ghetto, the lyrics from the Lower East Side where people only *thought* they knew how to speak or write English. If they couldn't speak the language, how could they write or versify in it? But they tried.

As Mrs. Cohen sat in her chair, little dark-haired Sammy with the big spectacles would begin to sing: "Ich bin a boarder from mine varb" – I'm a boarder at the house of my wife – "Manner is dis a tirin' job". (He's rhyming the English word "job" with the Yiddish word "varb".)

"Another incredible song I used to sing was 'Oy, I Like She', meaning 'Oh, I like her'. But that improved. 'Ir her Feesen und ir her Socken …' (In her feet and her socks …) 'I tell you pipple, it's no use talkin'.' The writer rhymes the English 'talkin'' with the Yiddish 'Socken'".

161

So Lets Hear The Applause

The original lyrics of "Bei Mir Bist Du Schon" were "Bei mir bist du schon, bei mir chostu chein" ("chein" is a Yiddish word meaning "charm"), "bei mir bist tu einer af der velt" (to me you are the only one in the world), "bei mir bist tu git – bei mir chostu *it*" (*it* being the word used to describe Clara Bow the *It Girl*, so he puts *it* in the lyric), "Bei mir bist du teire affen gelt" (To me you are more valuable than money) – what greater compliment could a Jewish boy pay a girl?

How Sammy got involved in that particular ditty comes a little later in the story.

Suffice it to say that the Yiddish melodies played in the Cohen household were not solely the wailings of impoverished exiles who put their fear of an inevitable pogrom into a piece of plaintive music.

But many of them sounded that way – because Sammy was tied to his mother not by the strings of her apron but by those of his violin. He hated the violin as much as he loved his mother. "In fact, I adored my mother – because she was the sort of person you could make a deal with," he explained.

The deal he made was that he would play the violin only up to the night of his barmitzvah – and not a minute later. Mrs. Cohen agreed – subject to an additional clause: he had to give a violin solo that night as a sort of swansong.

He played and went on to enjoy himself. At about 1 o'clock in the morning, his mother said: "Sam, we have to go pay the orchestra."

He was dumbstruck. "You mean", he asked her incredulously, "that these five guys get paid for having more fun all evening than everyone else here?"

"Sam," she replied, "they get paid."

Those four words opened up new vistas for 13-year-old Samuel Cohen that even he did not know existed. He sidled up to the bandleader and asked if they did that sort of thing often. "Yes," he was told, "all the time." In fact whenever the East Side or Brooklyn Jews had weddings or barmitzvahs and since someone always did, they worked.

Within a year, Sammy was working with them – in the

evenings; while during the day he walked around a kosher slaughter yard with a candle. He graded the meat and decided which cuts would go to the kosher butchers and which would be handed over to the non-Jewish traders. (Since there were certain parts of an animal – the hindquarters in particular – which were never kosher, this was not a particularly difficult job to do.)

It is not difficult to appreciate that Sammy was no more happy in the slaughter yard than he had been playing the violin in his parents' front parlour. And he was discovering he had a talent for writing songs. While still a teenager and working in a resort hotel with the same band who had played at his own barvitzvah, Sam scribbled both the words and music – and he says he hasn't written any music since – for a number called "Shake Your Head From Side to Side".

He also met a youth named Saul Caplan who made an arrangement of "Shake Your Head From Side to Side". Together they met a music publisher and with his father – because he was still a minor and couldn't complete a legal document – signed a contract. The song was a hit. He didn't give up playing with the band – his mother now acted as agent for the Jewish functions and he grew a moustache to make him look gentile enough to play at the hotels that didn't admit Jews – but he did chuck working in the slaughter yard.

Mrs. Cohen meanwhile still had other plans for him. With four sisters it was the only son's positive duty to become a doctor, lawyer or dentist. "I never made MD," he says slightly apologetically. "You see, it's an awesome responsibility being an only son. If a mother has five sons and two of them go to the chair and the other two are in Sing Sing, there is still hope that the other one will become a lawyer, dentist or doctor."

Sammy, by the way, had by this time become Sammy Kahn. He and Caplan wrote another song called "Rhythm Is My Business", had that one published and gleefully found that bandleader Jimmy Lunceford recorded it. When Sammy saw their names on the sheet music, he decided something had to be changed: "Kahn and Caplan looked like a Second Avenue dress firm," he explained. After much dithering, Caplan agreed to become Saul Chaplin and Sammy Kahn became Sammy Cahn.

Lunceford – who even got a "cut" of the writing action by agreeing to have his name in the credits, too – was playing at the Apollo Theatre in Harlem. The songwriting pair had been introduced to him by a youngster called Lou Levy. In the days when Sammy was a violinist, Levy was the son of the local greengrocer. He was, therefore, considered to be too low in station to ever catch up with the Cohens, ethnic ladder or no. Levy was now a black-face dancer specialising in the Lindy Hop, but he had the influence to introduce the pair to Lunceford. It was at the Apollo, too (although some time later), that Cahn first heard a couple of coloured singers performing "Bei Mir Bist Du Schon". Their names were Jimmy and George. "Imagine two black men singing in Yiddish – and that was way before Sammy Davis!"

The almost completely black audience was captivated and it was Cahn who thought how much more acceptable the tune would be if the people understood the words. He tried to get Tommy Dorsey to play the tune. He was laughed out of the Irishman's office.

But there is one thing you learn about Sammy Cahn very quickly. He doesn't give up. He met the Andrews Sisters who – because their ancestry was Greek – immediately thought that Bei Mir Bist Du Schon was a Greek song. That, anyway, is Cahn's story. He got them to record it and everything was going beautifully until Jack Kapp, head of Decca Records, discovered what they were doing – and decided very forcibly that he wasn't going to make a "race" record. He was one of those Jews who thought that anything Jewish was not only not commercial but not quite nice (although he was to modify that view and in 1948 persuaded Al Jolson not only to record the new State of Israel's national anthem "Hatikvah" but also to give away the proceeds to charity).

164

Cahn, however, persisted and wrote a new set of lyrics in English – and finally Kapp relented.

The rest of the story Sammy delights in telling to anyone who loves a tale about snatching a success from apparent disaster. In short what happened was that he went to meet a couple of Yiddish music publishers in Brooklyn – "Hell, I didn't go to Brooklyn when I was poor!" – twins whom he called "Tweedle Dum and Tweedle Dee, Tel Aviv style". They spoke alternate words of the sentence: "What – do – you – want?" After persuading them that what he wanted was the rights to the tune, they did a deal.

Everything was fine till Sammy returned from a Caribbean cruise which he had taken to celebrate the agreement – and found he was in the middle of a scandal. Newspapers were blaring the statement that he bought "a million dollars for 30 pieces of silver". The original writers of the piece, Sholem Secunda and Jacob Jacobs, were hopping mad – because they had sold the rights to the Brooklyn twins for $150. Warner Brothers, the publishers of the Cahn version, decided that the safe thing to do was to offer them two cents a copy. They accepted. Sammy received three quarters of a cent. "It sold 125,000 copies and I got three quarters of a cent for each of them. I wouldn't advise you to retire on that!"

But he could have retired a dozen times over on some of his other tunes – such as Doris Day's "It's Magic", Sinatra's "Come Fly With Me", "All the Way", "The Tender Trap", "High Hopes", "Love and Marriage", "My Kind of Town" and the Oscar-winning "Three Coins in the Fountain", Mario Lanza's "Be My Love", Bing Crosby's "The Second Time Around" and Julie Andrews's "Thoroughly Modern Millie".

How does he do it?

"I'll never forget meeting Cole Porter who was one of the most brilliant song writers of all time," he said. "You would have to toss a coin to see who made the biggest contribution to the popular song, Berlin or Cole Porter. But Porter told me: 'You know, I've always envied you!' Imagine, envied *me*!"

"Yes," he said, "I've always envied you that you were born on the Lower East Side. If I had been born there, I might have been a true genius."

Sammy is very proud of his Jewish heritage. He is not particularly religious, but come the High Holydays, he likes to find himself a synagogue and on Yom Kippur to fast as he had learned to do when he *was* on the East Side.

"I've spent the High Holydays in some very strange places," he recalled. "I was in Rio de Janeiro one Yom Kippur. I determined to fast and that I would get to the synagogue in time for the closing prayers and then hear the man blow the shofar.

"So I fasted and went to this beautiful temple in Rio. And the incredible thing is that the Jews in the temple were to all intents and purposes Brazilians. You wouldn't think they were Jews. They had this beautifully carved chair which they kept for honoured guests. And I sat in it and I turned to a man and spoke in Yiddish – which at moments like this becomes the common denominator: 'Well, I can't wait for the man to blow the shofar because I'm planning the most marvellous meal.' The man looked at me and said: 'We started the fast tonight.' I had fasted a day too early. So I turned to the ceiling and said to the Lord: 'You understood my intentions and they were purely honourable.' So I ate a night earlier, too!"

He doubtless also went back to writing another string of hits. And not necessarily the strictly commercial kind, either.

He is a specialist in parody. For John F. Kennedy's campaign he wrote a version of his "High Hopes" that went "K-E-double-N-e-d-y- Jack's the favourite guy. Everyone wants to back Jack. Jack is on the right track – and he's got high hopes."

He has been doing some of this work with George Barry, head of the Fabergé perfume empire. Asked how he liked working with the comparative amateur, Cahn told me: "Well he may not write as good as the others, but he sure smells better."

Once at a Fabergé occasion, he was asked to introduce, in song, Cary Grant. It went like this: "The most beautiful man in the world isn't me, no, isn't Dino, but as *we* know ... it's the man we honour today ... the most talented man in the world today is not John Gielgud, though he's real good, would he feel good ... if he had to do this for our friend Fabergé?"

A lot of these parodies-to-order he has done for Frank Sinatra – whom he has kept well enough stocked with the original thing.

In the summer of 1976 I asked him whether he had been to the recent Sinatra wedding. "No," he said. "It's much too hot there in the desert. And I'm not keen on Spiro Agnew. There was another reason, too – I wasn't invited."

A year later he was telling Jewish audiences, 'when they began with Begin ...'

On another occasion in 1983 he parodied his own "Thoroughly Modern Millie". It was appropriate – and said a lot about himself: "Everything tonight is thoroughly Jewish ..."

Bud Flanagan
(1896–1968)

Bud Flanagan

Underneath the Arches

They loved Bud Flanagan. Outrageous. Discourteous. Playful
– sometimes hurtful. He was the Royal Family's favourite
comic. A comedian who was Jewish. Never a Jewish comedian.

With his moth-eaten raccoon coat, the most famous straw
hat after Chevalier's – it always looked as though he had either
eaten it or used it as a seat – he only had to say "Oy" to have an
audience not so much sitting in his lap as metaphorically
licking his face like a contented dog. That was his secret. Other
showmen have made love to their audiences. Flanagan let their
love flood out to him. He sang "Underneath the Arches" or
"Maybe It's Because I'm a Londoner" and there was an
instant sense of poverty and a contentment with it.

Since his main audience in the early days was made up of
working class people who paid less than a shilling for a seat in
a music hall, it was a clever ploy.

His parents, who emigrated to London after personally
experiencing the horrors of a pogrom at Lodz in Czarist
Poland, would not have thought so. Chaim Reuven Weintrop
– for reasons no one has ever been able to adequately explain,
the reference books all list his name as originally being Robert,
not a nomenclature at all known in their environment – was
born in the heart of London's Jewish East End, in Spitalfields,
close to the fruit market, the Mazik Hadaas Synagogue and in
one of those tenements that smelled as much of stale salt
herring as of some of the other unpleasant manifestations of
slum life.

The year was 1896. It was the time when Jews streamed in
their millions out of East Europe for what they expected
would be the "goldener medena" – the golden land – of

America. The Weintrops were probably among the thousands unloaded unceremoniously at the London Docks in the fond belief they were in the United States. More than one family wandered the streets of the East End quite seriously imagining they were in New York. Chaim Weintrop made up that deficiency before very long. He found a job at one of London's most famous music halls, the Cambridge – where he was a callboy.

But that wasn't the position he aspired to in show business. At the age of 12 in 1908, he entered a talent contest at the Shoreditch Empire, the East End's "own" top music hall. He was, he told the theatre manager, a conjurer. He even had a name "Fargo, the Boy Wizard". It wasn't a good idea. His first trick was to turn water into wine – which another Jew is reputed to have tried and with more success. When that trick failed, he used all the assurance of youth – to say nothing of showmanship – to try something else.

"Is there a gentleman in the house who can lend me a bowler hat?" he asked innocently. "A bowler hat in Shoreditch!" he laughed years later. "There wasn't a bowler hat in the whole of the East End. Well, I couldn't do the trick with a cap – and I got the bird." Literally. In those days birds would be let loose to drown an unpopular act – somewhat kinder than the American habit of using a huge hook to drag acts off or a swinging weight to knock them down.

The toughest bird of all came from his father – who slapped him around the face, probably describing his actions as a "frusk in pisk". It was Friday night and the idea of working on Shabbos, the Sabbath, was even worse than the disgrace of attempting to entertain in one of those beer-swilling, smoke-laden houses of iniquity. "I dropped my bag of tricks in Shoreditch High Street," he was to recall. "And I ran."

That sort of experience makes young men and women of determination show their mettle. Chaim Weintrop could have stopped then and settled into the life of the East End, but he was ambitious and determined to get on.

It was an easier decision for a poor boy to make than

someone who was much more comfortably off. Apart from his parents and his heritage, he figured he had little to lose.

He was just past barmitzvah when he decided he had had enough. Chaim, too, had heard all the stories about the Promised Land of America and decided to see it for himself, but with a slightly different aim than his parents had had.

Not for him a search for a spot on God's earth where His praises could be sung in joy and without the fear of the Secret Police knocking on the door or Cossacks stampeding their way through the *shtetlach* – the small Jewish towns of the Pale of Settlement – burning their homes and raping their women. Even so soon after the turn of the century, there were stories about America being the home of show business.

He knew that ships to America left from Southampton. So he walked there. Once at the port, he said he was an electrician and obtained a job as a member of the crew. On his fourteenth birthday, the first day at sea, his ploy was discovered. He couldn't do a simple wiring job and so was consigned to the galley – about the worst thing that could happen short of being thrown overboard. For the length of the journey, he was washing up dishes, in between being seasick.

But he reached America. There were no problems with immigration and customs. He and another boy jumped on to the quayside and pretended to be porters carrying baggage. It got him into New York and a chance to walk through the streets of an area very like his own Spitalfields. He was on the Lower East Side, in Delancey Street, the nearest thing to an American Brick Lane – where he heard his name called. Incredible though it may have seemed, a fellow Londoner living there recognised him and got him a meal and a job as a Western Union messenger.

For a time Chaim Weintrop had a new name – as Luke McGlook, an English boxer. One round in the ring was enough to convince him that there were better ways to make a living. Instead, he sold newspapers on Broadway – as traditional a way of featuring in the rags-to-riches sagas as anyone had ever devised.

He was offered a job on the stage by one of the men buying a paper, and given a single line to say in the play *The Wild Beast*. From there he went to San Francisco with a school act, and then toured with it around Australia and New Zealand. They returned in time for the start of the First World War. A notice was pinned to the dressing room wall, suggesting it might be a good idea if all Englishmen rallied to the colours.

Chaim immediately returned home – and joined up. It turned out to be one of the most sensible things he ever did. It not only introduced him to the man who would be his stage partner for the next 30 years, but gave him a new name.

The name resulted from a less than cordial meeting with a sergeant. "He was the most Yiddified bastard I ever met," he recalled years later, remembering in the East End vernacular the degree of anti-Semitism to which he was subjected.

"Remember my name," the sergeant ordered on one occasion.

"Don't worry, mate," said Weintrop, "I'll never forget it." Neither he nor anyone else ever did forget Sgt. Flanagan.

Shortly after the war, the young but very experienced actor was walking in Piccadilly Circus and bumped into a fellow of about the same age whom he had casually met in the trenches in France. His name was Chesney Allen. He remembered Allen had described himself as an actor, a "pro". Later, they met again in the dressing room of Florrie Forde, a variety headliner. Allen was her business manager.

They decided to go into partnership. Flanagan and Allen were before long the most talked about act on the variety circuits. Bud, as he was now known, was the comic, Allen the straight man. Bud, in his coat and straw boater, the cockney with the high melodic voice, Allen slightly more "refined" as the audiences of the day would have noted, with a much deeper voice, and everywhere he went, a brown trilby.

"We complemented each other perfectly," Allen was to say. "He was Jewish. I, a Christian. Perfect combination."

The people out front thought so, too. They cheered the jokes, joined in songs like "The Umbrella Man", "Run Rabbit

Run" and, of course and inevitably "Underneath the Arches" which was just about the most popular signature tune/theme song of the inter-war years.

Eight years before the Second World War began, they joined Nervo and Knox, "Monsewer" Eddie Gray and Naughton and Gold to form the Crazy Gang. Chamber pots and wet fish became part of the routine together with a series of practical jokes on and off the stage that weren't always funny.

After the war, Ches — as he was always called — left the act through illness, although he was to outlive every other member of the gang. He nevertheless became Bud's manager. As the years went by, the names Flanagan and Allen remained part of British folklore, although Ches only joined Bud for a very occasional record — including a celebrated reprise of "Underneath the Arches" — or a Royal Variety Performance.

The Royal Family loved Bud's humour. They could be seen doubling over when he went to the footlights to ask the member of the audience whose car was causing an obstruction to move it. "The number," he said, is "HRH ..." It was enough. Early in the 1960s, he was a guest at a Buckingham Palace lunch at which he had difficulty explaining to Russia's first man in space, Yuri Gagarin that he wasn't personally a member of the Royal Family, although he did spend a lot of time in the Victoria Palace. His old father from Lodz would have enjoyed that.

Even George VI had been known to suggest gags to Bud. Once, the King saw the show and asked Bud in the interval: "Is this the show my daughter Margaret saw?"

"Yes, sir," said Flanagan, "but we did take a couple of the jokes out."

"You'd better put them straight back in again," said the King.

Later, when Bud received the supreme accolade, the medal of the Order of the British Empire at Buckingham Palace, he joked to Prince Philip: "This is a great house for a matinée."

Bud was always used to great houses, if not always to great news. It was while appearing on stage that he heard that his much-loved but greatly spoilt son Buddy was dying of leukaemia in Los Angeles. He left in the middle of the show and took the next plane to New York.

Unlike other showmen, Bud didn't live entirely for the theatre. When I met him towards the end of the Crazy Gang's time in 1962, he was much more concerned about the winner of the next race at Epsom. He was, in fact, one of the country's principal experts on what was once known as the sport of kings. He was frequently consulted by the racing tipsters of Britain's newspapers and when off-the-course gambling became legal in the 1960s, joined boxing promoter Jack Solomons in opening a chain of betting shops.

In 1968, at the age of 72, Bud Flanagan was dead. He probably never told a Jewish joke in his professional life. But everyone knew he was Jewish. There could be no better loved representative of his people.

Walter Matthau
(born 1920)

Walter Matthau

Retirement Actor

He was a crusty old man, with a stooped back, grey hair thinning on top and muttering insane remarks in a New York Jewish accent. At another time, from the same bent frame came a distinctly soft Middle-American voice. Later, the hair looked thicker, shiny and black and the back was straight. Thus Walter Matthau, now in his late 50s and one of the most consummate actors on the Hollywood screen, tackles his profession.

Had he not had George Burns as competition, chances are that Matthau (born Matuschanskayasky), son of a Lithuanian father and a Jewish mother, would have won an Oscar for his role as one of the two *Sunshine Boys*. Everything he said and did smacked of the Jewish vaudevillian that he in some ways still is. Like all professional entertainers, he is a man who is never entirely "off" – even though it took him nearly 30 years to reach the spotlight.

For all those years he was an actor in bit parts on the screen – including a hopefully forgotten supporting role with Elvis Presley – and on the stage. Two things changed that – he lost a fortune and he had a heart attack. Suddenly, recovery from both those near tragedies brought him the kind of success he had never before imagined possible.

I once met him for lunch. He had just been to his dentist so wanted something very smooth to ease his aching jaw. As we sat in the ultra-smart "Bistro" in Beverly Hills, he ordered vichyssoise followed by minestrone. When the waiter handed him the bill, he smiled and said, with the sort of irony that strikes home only with the last word and the blank expresison: "Lovely fellow. Used to be a lieutenant in the Gestapo!" From anyone else, it would have sounded offensive. Not from him.

As we walked out, he spoke about the violence in current entertainment. "You know, my mother watches television in her New York apartment with a knife in her hands. When she sees a crook come on the screen, she points her knife at him and says: 'If you come near me, I'll let you have it!'"

He talks a lot about his mother, mostly trying to demolish the myth that every Jewish son has the smell of his parents' chicken soup constantly under his nostrils. "My mother was a lousy cook," he insists. Which brought him to something else. "Can you give me a sentence containing the word judicious?" It was not a question you could possibly answer to his satisfaction – unless you had heard it before. "Kneidlach, kreplach and knishes are all Jew dishes."

As the comedian once said, it's not what you say, but the way that you say it. And Matthau has always been able to say it right – and in a variety of accents.

"Actually," he says, "I was always a swell guy ... shall I wait for the laugh? ... you know, you knock around for 20 years and suddenly you have a heart attack and then you become a movie star and it's all very funny. It's all a load of ... malarky."

He is not afraid of saying just how slow his climb to fame had been. "I'd say that in the first year I started acting, perhaps one in 10,000 in the local community knew who I was and each year it became less and less – one in 8,000; one in 6,000 until finally today it's perhaps one in 500 who knows who I am. Now, if one in every 500 people knows who you are, that's a lot of people."

One of the biggest problems about success for him has been the loss of his anonymity. "I long for the seclusion of my own thoughts and being able to do my own kind of day-dreaming," he says. "Today, I'm constantly on display. When I go out of the house, I hear people saying, 'Isn't that ... you know who ... the one who ...'"

He has never, of course, been a sex symbol in the way that the old matinée idols were or as Paul Newman, Ryan O'Neal or Robert Redford are today.

"I think I'm regarded as a sort of benevolent, old movie star who's slightly comical and doesn't appear in too many dirty pictures. I'm not a comedian. But some people expect me to be funny all the time. You know what I mean? You can spot them waiting for the bright remark and becoming more and more disappointed when it doesn't come." Surely, the lament of every clown who would rather play Hamlet, certainly of every comic who some time or other has been accosted by a complete stranger and ordered to "Say something funny".

Matthau says that he tries on occasions to live up to people's expectations. "I'm just an actor who seems to thrive in comedies which don't necessarily have to be funny," he explained. And the difference between comedy and tragedy? "Very simple," the way he sees it. "Tragedy is when the protagonist dies in the end. Comedy is when he doesn't."

The parts of Willie Clark in *The Sunshine Boys* and the dirty, untidy poker addict in *The Odd Couple* were straight out of the tradition of the Yiddish theatre – the *nebbichs* who believe the world owes them a living but who, at the same time, return a helping hand with a kick in the teeth.

They were both written by Neil Simon, the most successful (and Jewish) playwright of the 1970s. But they both needed an essentially Jewish actor to pull them off. Rather like telling a Jewish story. Only a Jew can really do it. Soon after making *The Odd Couple* Matthau told me: "I had done all the living I needed to do for that role. It came very naturally and easy for me – although that is not to say that I am naturally a sloppy or untidy person. Neither am I a neat person. Which reminds me of a story: A fellow gets married and the morning after the wedding night, goes to the bathroom and finds a dead horse in the bathtub. He runs out and says: 'Darling ... there's a dead horse in the bathtub.' To which his bride replies: 'Well, I never said I was neat.' "

Returning to the point he says: "I certainly know that kind of character. You play it with a sort of inner calm when you do know the man you are portraying. Then you feel happy."

180

Then he added, rather like Leo Rosten explaining one of his Joys of Yiddish: "the emotion of happiness is much smaller than the emotion of being miserable. That is why a lot of people like to lose when they gamble. They like to feel the larger emotion." That, after all, displays one of the essential characteristics of the Jew – who always enjoys a good cry providing the calamity is not too serious. An ingrowing toenail was a disaster but a pogrom was usually just one of those things that Jews had to live with through the generations.

Matthau was once a compulsive gambler, so he should know something about losing. The gambling fever ended at the same time as this heart attack began, or so he thought – like a member of Alcoholics Anonymous, a gambler is always a gambler and he would have recurring bouts of his "disease".

"I used to bet thousands – my yearly salary – on a game. I once lost 185,000 dollars in six weeks. It took me six years to recoup that money."

Losing the money had nothing like the effect on him of having a heart attack. "I suddenly saw myself in a mortal light," he said. "It had a tremendous effect on me. Before you have a heart attack, you think of yourself as immortal. But then suddenly I thought to myself: My God. This is how it happens. You can suddenly die in your sleep. You can't come back say: Wait a minute, I haven't finished everything. I'm right in the middle of the season. I can't die yet. You can – and you do."

It changed everything.

"I slowed down the intensity of my pursuits and speeded up the beauty and the healthy living part of my life. I work harder at the things that are more wholesome and delicious in life and less hard at the things that are frivolous, ridiculous and nonsensical."

An actor who has never been so busy in his life now considers himself to be a semi-retired performer (which probably distinguishes him from all the other Jewish entertainers). "What I do in films is retirement acting, you see. I give exhibi-

181

tions of my former skills. You can't really do acting in a film studio in the way you can on stage and then develop a character. On films you do a scene and then go back and do another that is supposed to be taking place 12 years hence. It's just ridiculous.

"It's bits and pieces and snatches of acting. A little bit here and a little bit there. Characterisation number six here; characterisation number 14 there. No one can call that real acting."

It is an unusual definiton of the film actor and his craft. But he does say that retirement acting comes easier if you are a success.

"The average actor has to work his ass off just to stay alive. It's the hardest work in the world if you're not on top. You not only have to use your body and your sweat. You also have to use your blood – because an actor is totally naked in order to work. He has to open his guts."

And he then confirmed the difference about being a Jewish actor. "An actor *has* to be able to show his background in his work, his genetic and environmental structure. He has to show not just what he is but what he has been. He has to show his aspiration and his fears. If you don't do that, you are not a real actor at all."

There's a dry humour about Walter Matthau, a humour honed by the 20 years before he became almost a household name – he still is convinced that most people don't know who he is. At the age of 27 he played the "oldest and wisest man" in the kingdom in a version of *Anne of the Thousand Days*, starring Rex Harrison. "I had to say 'I have known you from a child, King Harry. I was present when you took your first three steps ....' Harrison turned his back on the audience and said: 'Oh, sh—!'"

There is something of the old ghetto Jewish attitude to life in his own acceptance of the rather woebegone old-before-his-time Matthau appearance. As he told me: " I always *thought* I looked like Olivier and it was stupid of audiences not to recognise it."

Sophie Tucker
(1887–1965)

Sophie Tucker

Yiddisher Mama

She was the woman in the expensive long gowns who always clutched a handkerchief in one hand and had a devoted public clinging to the other. At the age of 75 she was still giving advice to other "girls" about their lovers and still weeping over her lost childhood.

Sophie Tucker was the Last of the Red Hot Mamas – although no one had ever heard of the first – and the devoted daughter of her own Yiddisher Mama. A legend that was larger than life and as big as her own bulk.

She was a contradiction, a paradox. "Who Wants Them Tall, Dark and Handsome?" she asked in one song. In another she bemoaned the fact that "Nobody Loves a Fat Girl". Yet Sophie Tucker was widely loved by the audiences she manipulated so adroitly and for her incredible generosity.

"I never say no to a benefit," she boasted. "Especially for my own people."

She once sang a song called "My People" about the Jews to whom she had felt so close ever since the days when she helped her parents run a small kosher restaurant at Hartford, Connecticut. Yet in the East of London in 1936 she could fake a demonstration against her by a group of fascists – because she knew it would spell publicity, a commodity as vital to her as the love of an audience.

Her most popular song, always performed partly in English, partly in Yiddish – "My Yiddisher Mama" – made Sophie herself into a mother figure. Yet she deserted her own son Bert when he was still a baby for the lure of bright lights which she was convinced were beckoning just about 100 miles away on Broadway.

184

Sophie Tucker

More than anything else, she wanted people to like her. But she knew neither how to show gratitude nor how to apologise.

A gruff word or nod were the nearest ways she knew of saying thank you, in person. But when people acknowledged a gift that she had sent them, she would send another letter thanking them for thanking her.

She was one of The Generation, part of the scene that governed the way Americans in particular spent their precious moments of leisure. While the men pulled themselves up by their own bootlaces, Sophie dragged herself from the slums with a pull at the strings of her corset.

Like so many of her contemporaries, she at first worked in black-face. But she was always afraid people would think this made her less Jewish – although most of the other black-face stars and practically all the men who wrote songs about the South were, too.

"I'm a Jew and there's nothing renegade about me," she once declared. "God is good to the Jewish. Sarah Bernhardt is a Jew. I was black-face most of the afternoon and white-face by night. Nobody would believe that a Jew would do black-face. Not even when I rolled up my sleeve and showed a white arm. There must be something unJewish about my features when the cork is on."

Not really. She wrote to her father in Yiddish, although the words came to her much more slowly than her rendering of "Yiddisher Mama" later on would convey. Once when she took her aged and proud mother back to her old school at Hartford the old lady was astonished at her leading the children in a spirited version of "Onward Christian Soldiers". Her reply was not exactly aimed at promoting race relations.

"What do I care if they all fight and kill each other?" she said.

She might have continued her black-face act had not her luggage got lost one day leaving her no choice but to appear on stage without the burnt cork.

After that, managements were no longer sure how to receive her. She couldn't claim to be a "coon shouter". A new designa-

185

tion had to be found for the young, ambitious Miss Tucker. She called herself "The Mary Garden of Ragtime" – after a popular opera star of the era. She kept the name until Mary Garden was forgotten. By then, she thought it appropriate to be billed as "The Last of the Red Hot Mamas".

The maternal image seemed to be appropriate, especially since she didn't let too many people into the know about Bert. At one time, he was going to appear on stage with her, but she thought better of it after he had a sudden illness.

Pretending to be a good mama on stage was just another polite fiction that her audience expected. She was well over 50 before she started singing "Life Begins at 40" – but by singing the song she not only had a new number, she was also buying an insurance policy and making a bid for the audiences who could by then have started drifting away. When she realised that this was paying off, she organised a club – for the over 40s telling them her beauty secrets and how impossible she found it to diet. She had the women feeling like soul sisters and the men were given another excuse for an extra indulgence.

She worked harder and longer than almost any other entertainer in the history of show business because after a time she knew no other way. Money was a mere measure of success. She craved high salaries because when she got them, her contemporaries would know how much she was worth – in the same way that she wanted to impress the ladies in her old home town by fulfilling her own prayer: "Lord, make me a headliner."

Sophie Tucker became that headliner – sometimes in three completely different shows in different places on the same evening. But she paid for that incredible success by never knowing how to live.

On one occasion at a Passover dinner in Israel, she and Golda Meir chewed the matzo fat over their past, recalling, first, mutual experiences in Milwaukee, second, bemoaning the sacrifices they had made in their home lives. For Sophie Tucker it was no sacrifice. She went into it with her eyes wide open and her arms outstretched – begging to be taken away from Hartford and into the Big Time.

In her early days she even toyed with going on to the streets – if that way she could earn enough to keep her in New York. A kind policeman and a café proprietor who recognised that her talent extended beyond the bedroom saved her from that impulse – and she went on to incredible riches.

Tucker was not her real name any more than were the stage names of the rest of the members of The Generation. She was born Sophie Kalish – although by the time she was taken to the United States as a babe-in-arms her mother had discovered that that was not right either.

Her father had escaped from the Czar's Army and on the way to America had "borrowed" the name of an Italian who died on the voyage, one Charles Abuza.

His wife Jenny had given birth to the girl she called Sophie in a farmhouse on the way to the Baltic coast, somewhere near the Russian-Polish border.

It was an omen for the future, a pattern for the way in which the adolescent and adult Sophie would work – in a hurry.

The name Abuza stuck, both to the family and to the restaurant where nothing cost more than 25 cents – that is, unless you wanted a steak, chicken or duck with vegetables and dessert; then, you paid 50 cents.

Sophie washed dishes, scrubbed floors, waited on table and sang for other people's suppers. The place was popular with touring vaudeville artists, among them a couple known as the Howard Brothers, Willie and Eugene. They suggested she should try her luck in show business and the best place to do it they said was in New York. But it was not as easy as it seemed. By the time she was 18, Sophie had married a brewery cart driver called Lewis Tuck and had given birth to her son. By the time that baby was no more than a year old, Tuck had already left her. So Sophie persuaded her younger sister Annie to take charge of the child and with a note, left for Mama and Papa, went looking for the bright lights.

The usual disappointments followed the usual knocks on doors of agents' offices and the unusual spells watching the handbag-twirling girls, whom she nearly joined, standing on street corners.

Finally, Sophie found a job singing and that led to another which in turn led to another. She became firmly entrenched first in burlesque and then in vaudeville. She would have made it in the Very Big Time had it not been for the undoubted jealousy of established stars such as Nora Bayes – who came before The Generation – and Eva Tanguay, who by virtue of birth could never have been part of it.

Sophie had a solo spot in the most lush entertainment of its day, the Ziegfeld Follies. But the stars, the Misses Bayes and Tanguay, suspected she would be taking too much applause away from them and had her fired.

She went back to vaudeville, met William Morris, head of the famous agency bearing his name and at that time the proprietor of his own vaudeville circuit.

As a result she could enjoy what she always regarded as her greatest triumph – going back to Hartford and impressing the neighbours by buying her mother a fur coat. She sent her younger brother Moe to college, helped her elder brother into business as her manager, paid for her sister Annie's wedding. But Bert represented her conscience – and one that she was never really willing to admit existed.

She sent him away to military school and told her friends and herself what a good mother she had been to do so. When he sent her Jewish New Year cards to the "most wonderful mother in the world " she pasted them into the same scrapbook in which she recorded the cost of an hotel room.

It could be argued that she was no better wife than she was a mother, but it also has to be admitted she had her share of bad luck experiences. Lewis Tuck left her and then died – although she all but kept his name. Her second husband Frank Westphal was a piano player who was insanely jealous of her success; but instead of helping him to adjust, she bought him a car repair business which she insisted on calling the Sophie

Tucker Garage – "it would be good for business" she argued. The third "Mr. Tucker" was Al Lackey, a little man with a Napoleonic complex, a sometime clothing salesman and business manager who became a professional gambler. She spent as much time bailing him out of debt as she did arranging her own career.

From vaudeville Sophie became the Nightclub Queen, all the time adding a bit of fantasy here, a downright lie there – if it appeared to further her business prospects. She told the world she had entertained the Queen of the Netherlands long before she had ever even left her own country. But in 1934, on one of the first of what were to become her regular visits to the London she loved, she stopped the show at the Royal Command Performance by looking up to the Sovereign's box, saluting and shouting: "Hiya, King." It wasn't easy to get away with a greeting like that, but Sophie could.

If she wanted letters from the Royal Family which she could then add to her scrapbook and then inform the Press, she sent *them* presents – because she knew she would receive a reply.

But she was the most generous performer of them all. Whenever she had a record album on sale, the profits automatically went to charity. When she published her own autobiography at the end of the Second World War, *Some of These Days*, a whole string of charitable causes benefited.

She used for the name of the book the title of her second most famous song – brought to her by a young composer called Shelton Brooks in 1910. It was her uncanny judgement of what was and what was not right for her that helped make that song an international success and made Mr. Brooks a fortune. But her stubbornness nearly prevented it happening at all. She refused to meet the song writer at her dressing room door, and it was only on the insistence of her coloured maid, Mollie, that she show some good manners that finally and reluctantly she agreed to do so.

She was living proof that you could reach the top without bothering with hit parades or other people's ideas of fashion. Very few of her songs became standards for anyone else –

simply because she rarely sang tunes that people found themselves whistling on their way out of the nightclubs or the theatres where she worked. When she did record other people's material, the results were far from happy – she always seemed to be struggling too hard to escape from her stereotype. Yet even at the age of 75, she could dress up as a cowboy and twirl a gun that rotated almost as fast as her chins.

She could sing risqué songs that brought blushes to local do-gooders; yet tell her a dirty joke and she would show you the door. She could give millions of dollars away to charity yet baulk at paying more than a ten-cent tip to a hotel porter.

She was to say that her marriages cost her a million dollars. She was a failure as a mother, but she also feared that she was a failure as a woman, too; hence her constant efforts to prove things to herself. In a poker game she would keep up with the boys in her business team and play for higher stakes than they were sometimes willing to gamble. But when she lost, she was not always quite as ready to pay up as she expected them to be.

She invested her money wisely – taking a tip from William Morris who kept telling her: "Soph, buy dirt." She bought acres of ground on which were to grow some of the most valuable office buildings in the country.

To some, Sophie remained intensely honourable. Particularly to the people who worked for her for years but who never called her anything but "Miss Tucker".

Piano player Ted Shapiro was one. He was placed on salary when he first met Sophie, was never given a contract or a letter of appointment, yet stayed with her for 43 years. All through that time whether he was needed or not, his "Miss Tucker" paid him his salary – even when she worked in Hollywood in one of a series of ill-conceived forays into the world of motion pictures which both she and her fans were to regret. She had no need of a piano player to work with the orchestras that were put at her disposal, but Shapiro received his money regularly each week – as well as another cheque from Warner Brothers as "technical adviser", a job he was never called upon to fulfil.

Another salary – ten per cent of everything she earned – went to the man who wrote "Yiddisher Mama" and a whole catalogue of other hits, Jack Yellen. Even when she was asked at the last minute to perform at a private party about which Yellen could never possibly have known anything, she paid him the same ten per cent that he received as his share of her nightclub or stage earnings.

It was difficult keeping up with Sophie's work schedule. As we have seen already, she revelled in a variety of business activities. In London in the late '20s she could be performing for the Prince of Wales at his private apartments *after* having given two shows at the famous Kit Cat Club, another two at the Victoria Palace music hall and one at the Duke of York's Theatre. The following Sunday she might be experimenting with Greek drama – playing Socrates's mother in a special performance for a theatre club.

While in London she thought it would be good publicity to be reported as rescuing an eight-year-old boy from under the wheels of a car. A willing boy and car were both found, Sophie got herself into position and surprise, surprise, the event just happened to be reported in almost every newspaper in Britain and America.

Just as she could generally pick good material for herself, Sophie also displayed fairly good judgment when it came to spotting other people's talent. Here, she was almost as generous as she was with her money. She worked to promote the career of Gilda Grey who became well-known as the "Shimmy Queen" and pulled out all the stops while making a picture called *Broadway Melody of 1938* to give most of the credit to a teenager called Judy Garland. Years later, she dreamed of Judy playing herself in a film she desperately wanted to be called *The Sophie Tucker Story*. But it never happened – although she worked to place Betty Hutton in the role if she couldn't get Judy. Eventually, she had to content herself with a Broadway show called *Sophie*, which in the early 1960s unfortunately took off like a lead balloon.

To mark her 50 years in show business in 1953, the City of

San Francisco showed their appreciation of her amazing career that had found her a place among the immortals. The citation for a special award presented by San Francisco Mayor Elmer E. Robinson declared: "San Francisco, a high spirited warm-hearted city, hails and salutes Sophie Tucker, a high-spirited and warm-hearted lady who is America's first lady of show business. For 50 years, Sophie Tucker's radiant personality has won her a special place in the affections of the American people. May she enjoy many more years of bringing happiness to others; may that happiness return to her a hundred fold."

Cities took to Sophie Tucker as she herself took to diamonds and furs. Chicago was like a second home to her, even during the Al Capone gang war era. On one occasion, a gangster called her with the warning: "Don't wear your ice tonight, Soph." The result was that she was taken to the theatre that night with a police escort – while her diamonds stayed in the hotel safe. Later, the gangster who made the call phoned to explain why he had been so insistent. "We all love Sophie here," he said, "besides the other guys came from out of town."

They loved her both out of jail and inside. Year after year she gave concerts in prisons and spent fortunes on organising for the inmates anything from Christmas dinners to Passover seders. They, in turn, showed their gratitude by making her comforts and toys.

Although indifferent to her own son Bert, she showered love and affection on those people who either paid to see her perform or who for various reasons got in free. During the 18 months of America's involvement in the First World War, she collected thousands of dollars with which to buy tobacco to send to the men in the trenches.

In World War Two she toured Army hospitals, but wasn't able to visit as many of the camps as she would have liked – because William Morris advised that the base chaplains might complain about her salty material.

She had her ups and downs but was rarely out of the public

eye, partly because of her insatiable thirst for publicity and partly because of her incredible stage presence.

One critic wrote: "A bubbling mound of pastel pink and sequins, she attacks her audience like a bulldozer gone berserk. Her pudgy arms beat the air, her raucous voice pins your ears back and her body quivers like a minor earthquake."

"Minor" earthquake? There was nothing minor about Sophie – apart from the key in which she sang her songs and which brought just as many tears to her eyes as to those of her audiences. She was always in complete control of her act – and heaven help any supporting players who took up her valuable stage time.

When she celebrated her golden jubilee as a performer it was appropriately the Jewish Theatrical League that gave a dinner in her honour.

"I'm older than hell," she said then, "but I've never felt better," and then proceeded to read a poem she had concocted for the occasion:

> Success, is it really fame and gold?
> You won't know the answer till you're old
> And look down the road where the years have fled
> Then up the little stretch that lies ahead ...
>
> Not with gold and with glory will my trunk be packed
> When the Big Booker up yonder closes my act
> All I'll take with me then will be the souvenirs
> Of the real gold in my golden 50 years.

It was corny as anything she had ever recited on stage – and she had long since lost the ability to sing in tune – but it summed up the way a lot of people felt.

She was not going to let the "Big Booker up yonder" close any act when she felt there were people ready to hear her.

Time was when she would stand on a theatre's stage or in the midst of a crowded nightclub and belt out "Some of theeez dayayays ... you're gonna miss mea ... honeeee ...." Now she spoke the words, but she was every bit as effective.

As late as 1962, she was the biggest sensation of all at yet another Royal Command Performance – which proved not only her staying power but her ability to keep up with the times without having to be of them.

Sophie said that her next step would be Cape Canaveral where she was going to train with the spacemen. There was one trouble, however: "I don't think they've got a rocket powerful enough to lift me off the ground."

Above all, Sophie loved being with the contemporaries she respected so much and who she knew returned that respect. With Maurice Chevalier she could perform the "I Remember It Well" number from *Gigi* which had been so beautifully rendered in the film by that British Jewish character comedienne Hermione Gingold. M. Chevalier was delighted. As he once told me: "She was always so good. A little bit fat, but very attractive."

It was a genuine compliment. Thirty years earlier, he had told her: "I think you are the most wonderful artist of your kind that I have ever seen."

She could also give advice to youngsters who were hoping to one day step into her own beaded slippers.

"The kids in show business lack something we all had – the combination of humility and push ... the feeling of humbleness and the wish to do the things that have to be done, to learn by hard, hard grinding work the things that get you up on top and keep you there."

As she said, she put herself in lights. She claimed to have done it without the help of a press agent, which was hardly true. The importance of her press activities finally came to light in the early 1950s – when her entire collection of hundreds of scrapbooks was donated to the New York Public Library.

It represented no more than a shadow of the life of one of show business's greatest characters – who died, a shadow herself, from cancer early in 1966. The Last of the Red Hot Mammas? Only a personality as strong as Sophie could be so cool about that designation.

Steven Spielberg
(born 1946)

Steven Spielberg

ET and a Jewish Mother's Dream

Steven Spielberg is every Jewish mother's favourite son — which is reason enough to justify his position in a book about Jewish entertainers.

All right already, so he hasn't *yet* married a nice Jewish girl. And if he doesn't do a song and dance act on the stage, is that reason to leave him out?

No, it plainly isn't. He is just about the richest director in Hollywood and at the time of writing was very much the right side of 40. And if he is disappointed that he hasn't had to order a new sideboard for his Oscars — for some reason the Academy of Motion Picture Arts and Sciences doesn't share the popular taste — well, there *are* compensations.

He is the man reputed to have notched up something like a million dollars a *day* with his film about the space-age teddy bear *ET, the Extra-Terrestrial*, which he made when he was 35.

If that seems to place too much emphasis on his age, then it should be realised that he had already given us *Close Encounters of a Third Kind* which was a new kind of sci-fi production. For the first time, invaders from outer space were not portrayed as being about to imperil the American way of life. But it wasn't the first time he had made himself a millionaire from a movie.

It followed on a little thing called *Jaws* which had established him as a director who not only knew one end of a camera from the other, but had a gift for sizing up the potential of the box office, too.

All this is such a success story that when he didn't get the

Oscar everyone expected for *Raiders of the Lost Ark*, Hollywood society members scratched their heads and wondered whether he would be so angry he would be unable to create anything new.

ET was the answer – the biggest cult activity since McDonalds (you should forgive the expression) first went into the fast-food business.

To demonstrate just how new Spielberg is on the scene, it was his *father* who was a computer scientist – a job in most Jewish success stories restricted to grandsons. His mother, however, fits beautifully into the Borsht Belt stereotype.

She runs a deli – strictly kosher, yet – called the Milky Way in Los Angeles and while her little Steve is playing around with his cameras and editing machines, she is involved with the much more serious business of showing just how blintzes should be made, not too much pastry, not too much cheese, perhaps just a little bit of love thrown in.

Leah Adler claims to make the best kosher lasagne her side of the Rome ghetto. And although there can be no question of mixing her milk dishes with meat, at home she can produce the one panacea for all Steven's health problems (as a boy he looked as if he could do with an UNWRA food parcel): her chicken soup.

"It's Jewish penicillin," says Steve in one of the only unoriginal statements credited to this most original of film makers.

It is his father Arnold Spielberg whom he blames for his joint obsessions – the cinema and astronomy. When he was three years old in 1949, he was awakened by Arnold in the middle of the night to drive off to a field where the whole neighbourhood appeared to be gathering to watch a parade of meteors in the night sky. It is a scene that has been acted out again and again in Spielberg films.

At about the same time, Arnold and Leah took him to see the Charlton Heston circus epic *The Greatest Show on Earth*.

It was his very first movie. "It's going to be bigger than you," his father warned him before he took his hesitant steps into the darkness. "But don't worry. The people in it are going to be up there on the screen and they can't get at you."

That, of course, was where Spielberg Senior was all wrong. The people up there on the screen have been getting at him ever since.

It affected him first via the home-movie camera – and always with his mother's total approval. She knew her boy was going to make something of himself. And if he asked her to fill her best pressure cooker with cherries and just wait for the explosion so that he could film it all splattering the kitchen walls like a massive boil discharging, then there had to be a good reason for it. Religions have been built on less – but then if a Jewish mother's adoration for her son isn't a religion, what is?

When they went out for a day's outing in the family car, it was Steven who would take the cine camera along with him for the ride. The family would comb their hair, adjust their faces and look expectantly at the camera lens – which was whirring continuously, focussed on the moving car's hub caps. Steven knew what he was doing, so who was Leah to argue?

His first feature length film lasted for two and a half hours. It was shot in eight-millimetre. Professionally, his debut came with a short called *Amblin*, about a couple of kids hitch-hiking through the Mojave Desert. He later called it a "Pepsi commercial". Commercial it was – but not for Pepsi. What it sold was Steven Spielberg. The film went on release throughout the United States with the big 1970-blockbuster *Love Story* and had a happier ending.

As a result, in his early twenties, he won a contract with Universal, directing TV films. His first star – Joan Crawford, already well down the slippery slope to the end of her career making a *Night Gallery* episode.

Other TV spots followed with editions of *Columbo* and *Marcus Welby, MD*.

Then came a chance to make a "Movie of the Week", intended as a top prime-time television film which would keep the schedules filled but was almost certainly guaranteed for oblivion thereafter, particularly in so-called artistic circles. That was when Steven Spielberg proved that he was different from most other TV people.

This story about a motorist haunted by an unseen truck driver with a maniacal desire to consign him to the nearest ditch seemed to a lot of people to represent the struggle of man against the age in which he lives.

Dennis Weaver was chased constantly by the truck for no reason he could fathom. It tried to drive him off the highway, into the path of oncoming traffic, into every conceivable avenue leading to a fiery, painful death. It was a masterly example of directing and film cross-cutting – and led to the sort of offers other people in his business dream of.

There followed *The Sugarland Express* with Goldie Hawn, and then *Jaws* and the others. None of it bad for a man who tried without success to get into a cinema school – his grades weren't considered good enough. That is the sort of failure to be envied.

His film *Poltergeist* – which he described as his revenge on television – alone would have won him a scholarship. Now he has to content himself with people long in the tooth in the film business, coming to him for advice on how he manages to do it all.

Flops? Well, there was an indulgence called *1941*, a fantasy about the time Los Angeles thought it was about to be invaded by the Japanese. For anyone else, it would have been the end of an amazingly brief career. Spielberg was in the position to simply take a look at his drawing board and start all over again. It didn't take long before the money and the Oscars came crowding in.

He says he owes it all to his parents. Of his mother, he says: "From the time I was a child I always saw *her* as a performer. There was always something dramatic going on around her. I know the neighbours thought we were weird."

As the man said, that weird, we should all be.

Larry Adler
(born 1914)

Larry Adler

Mouth Organ Magic

He's a little man with long wiry fingers. When he stands on stage or in the middle of a cabaret floor, he doesn't look too unlike the old fashioned microphones which used to dominate theatres before pop singers were strangled by cables. Or perhaps an aeroplane with its propeller spinning would be a better description.

Larry Adler was the boy genius who taught the world to respect the instrument which everyone thought was good only for school playgrounds and street corners. He gave dignity to the mouth organ.

These days Adler is still doing what he did as a kid, although he is now close to his 70th birthday and plays the typewriter, the knife and fork and the chat show mikes almost as much as he does the mouth organ. You won't catch him calling it a harmonica, by the way. "It deserves the dignity of standing up for itself, so I say loudly and clearly *mouth organ*," he told me on our first meeting. That was in 1962. Since then I have interviewed him about a dozen times – in my BBC radio programme studio and in his bathroom as he fought for words with a sponge and a piece of soap. I imagine that is the only way to prevent him from talking, a pastime he obviously enjoys most. Unless you count the mouth organ itself – or a fine example of French or Italian cuisine. In recent years he has been restaurant critic for *Harpers* and *Queen*.

In between our more formal interviews he had published a less than kind (it had been changed in editing, he assured me) review of one of my books in the *Sunday Times* and we had bumped into each other casually in two or three places. "To forgive me that review", he said, "for a Jew you are a very Christian gentleman."

Adler is an interesting man (even if his taste in books is suspect). Most interesting of all, of course, is what he did for the mouth organ – and what the mouth organ did for him. It is, he readily admits, an instrument with "built-in prejudice".

In Germany, they once refused to allow him to play Bach. In Helsinki, the head of the radio service made a formal announcement to the press that Adler would perform the composer's works on a mouth organ over his dead body.

The real problem, he concedes, is that the little mouth organ needs a big microphone. "It has no amplification and while my friend Isaac Stern never needs a microphone when he plays, I always do."

It was at the age of five that the twin delights of show business and music first struck young Larry Adler. His grandfather ran a dairy –· which made him a sort of Tevya from Baltimore. His father was a plumber. Both were Orthodox. But somehow or other, Larry got to see within a short space of time both Serge Rachmaninov and Al Jolson. Both made a deep impression.

But he was 14 before he did anything about merging those two influences into one career for himself.

The *Evening Sun* newspaper organised a mouth organ contest. Larry taught himself to play and won the competition. Three months later, he made the Big Decision – to run away from home.

There were two main reasons for the break: "I hated school and loathed Baltimore." At school, he had suffered from a continuous tirade of anti-Semitism. "I was either being called Christ-killer or Jew bastard." Baltimore itself was an "overoppressive ghetto".

During those weeks between winning the contest and running away, he had to fight the prejudices of his home. "My relationship with my parents was what I thought a good Jewish family should be. But I was never embraced by my parents – and as a result I always made a big point of having plenty of physical contact with my own children. My grandfather warned my father about the evil ways I'd get into if he let me go on the stage. I would become syphilitic, narcotic and homosexual and I would destroy my lungs from smoking – all in a six-months curriculum."

The example of another nice Jewish Baltimore boy was also thrust before him by his grandfather. Shura Cherkassky at the age of eight was a prodigy on the piano. Grandpa used to tell his father: "Look at Shura Cherkassky. He's giving recitals already. What is *he* doing? *He's* a bum!" *He* being Larry. As it turned out, Larry was going to stick to the mouth organ – mainly because he wasn't any good at the piano. He had already been expelled from the Peabody Conservatory because he was "hopeless".

He says, in fact, that had he been born a White Anglo-Saxon Protestant he would never have taken up music at all. "I might have become a civil engineer." Not that he really ever intended to become a civil engineer, he points out. Simply that Jews were banned from the Baltimore college that trained civil engineers and this inflamed his sense of injustice. "And there seemed no racial discrimination in music."

In those days, he kept himself Orthodox and spent at least two years trying to stay kosher.

He stuck to those principles through the length of an ill-fated Fred and Adele Astaire show presented by Florenz Ziegfeld, called *Smiles*. Nobody like the songs, the book or the man who wrote it, William Anthony McGuire. So the stars used to console themselves at the famous 21 Club speakeasy. One night the Astaires and the beautiful Marilyn Miller took Larry with them. He chose two boiled eggs.

He abandoned those principles – and stopped going to synagogues whenever he could – when he said to himself: "Try to find a kosher restaurant in Iowa." But he added: "I became a better Jew when I stopped being religious." It was then that he thought more about the Jewish heritage, became a fervent Zionist and when he was considered important enough to play for charity benefits, chose Jewish causes before others.

"I am not, incidentally, a Jewish person, a Jewish fellow or a Jewish boy. I'm a Jew."

Before the irreligious Jew found himself, however, he had to find work. He ran away to New York because for a young boy from Baltimore there was nowhere else to go. He had a little money – "because I had been selling *Liberty* magazines in my spare time."

All he wanted to do was to join an outfit known as Borrah Mennevitch and his Harmonica Rascals. Mr. Minnevitch however, had other ideas. He heard Adler play and told him: "Kid, you stink."

Larry was on his way back to Baltimore when he saw a sign advertising a talent show that had Rudy Vallee – the first of the crooners – as its star M.C. Vallee wasn't that impressed, but Larry stayed on to get a better reception from the man who took over as M.C.

He was given his chance, plus a salary cheque of $100 every week. For a boy of 14 in 1928 that was huge money.

"I did it for 44 weeks and for 44 weeks learned my trade." He followed it with another season – earning now $150 a week. "I thought that was how show business went. You followed one contract with another, all the time getting $50 raises."

It didn't happen quite like that, however. He didn't get another contract and was then out of work. When he did find work it was to accompany a performing bear at $50 a week. Borrah Minnevitch came to see him – not to offer work, but to gloat.

But things were to look up. He became one of the Gus Edwards nursery of performers, where he was seen by Eddie Cantor. Cantor liked what he saw and hired him for his own show – to play a telegram boy.

Eddie was at the height of his fame and in the midst of a concerted campaign in which he was constantly teased for fathering five daughters and no sons. He used to say: "When I want a boy I send for Western Union." Adler, with his thin slight frame and big eyes was frequently said to look like the great star. In this show, he had to follow Cantor's joke about Western Union by appearing in the telegram company's uniform. Eddie would look at his features, ask him his age and the place where he was born. Larry would say "Baltimore", Eddie would count dates on his fingers and say: "Nineteen fourteen .... I was in Seattle. It couldn't be."

He was more than Larry's boss. He was his mentor and guardian. "He made sure I wrote home regularly and that I had proper meals," Adler recalls affectionately.

From Cantor, he became known as *the* mouth organ virtuoso. In the mid '30s he went to Hollywood – not to make a film but to play at Grauman's Chinese Theatre, the cinema which is more famous for its foyer than its films. It is there that the stars' footprints are preserved for posterity in cement.

While in the film capital, he was signed for a picture called *Many Happy Returns* and then for another that was due to be made by Walter Wanger, but never was. In 1937, he made *Singing Marines* and then in quick succession *Music for Millions, Three Dancing Daughters* and *St. Martin's Lane.*

He wasn't really a film person, but being there it was difficult not to become part of Hollywood – a town that not only made films but also had a substantial intellectual, political community.

In 1947, he became one of the members of the Committee for the First Amendment –a group that met in Ira Gershwin's home and included among its number Danny Kaye, Gene Kelly, John Huston, John Garfield and Humphrey Bogart.

In protest against the murderous investigations of the Un-American Affairs Committee soon to be headed by the infamous Senator Joe McCarthy – and its hounding of Hollywood writers, the Committeee for the First Amendment hired a plane and flew to Washington. Soon after the hearings closed for a break, the papers took up where McCarthy and his friends had left off. The film stars' committee was hounded to the point where one by one – Bogart being the first – they severed their connections. Adler decided to stick to what he considered to be his principles.

He had for a long time been linked with left-wing causes, but he says he was never a member of the Communist party. "It never interested me. I am not the sort of person who could take orders from a central committee, whether it be an Ortho-dox synagogue or a Communist party. I was asked for details about the political membership of Hollywood writers and I just told the committee it was none of their goddam business."

As a result, he was placed on two black lists, by both the American Legion and the Hearst newspaper chain. Work became more and more difficult to obtain, and by 1950 it had dried up altogether.

The only thing he says he now regrets about his actions during that period was suing a woman writer for libel. "Suing a lady for libel made me a villain who was prosecuting a brave American who was fighting Communism. I should have sued the Hearst papers instead."

With no work in his native United States, Adler came to Britain where he has virtually stayed ever since. The only problem he had with work in England was when Val Parnell received a batch of hate mail at the London Palladium. But it did not stop him working.

And that work expanded from the stage of cinemas and vaudeville theatres to concert halls throughout the world – and since 1959 back to America itself. He was very unsure about returning to the States. The prejudice was still very obvious in the early '60s, but it was to vanish completely by the end of the decade. Throughout this time, he has remained an American citizen "because when I open my mouth, you know what I am. But I just could never live there. My roots are American and I'd like to stay American. But America has lost all its fun, all its excitement. It's blander than it was. I just don't like what has happened to the country. There is a tremendous apathy about almost everything."

Staying American has curtailed the lengths to which he has

been able to take some of his political activities in the United Kingdom. He has been active in the campaign for prison reform. He is outspoken about apartheid and refuses to play in South Africa because mixed audiences are still prohibited.

He has never, however, refused to play in Germany. "I don't believe you can indict a whole nation," was how he put it to me at our very first meeting. It was not something his friend Isaac Stern could understand at that time.

One of his earliest appearances in Germany was soon after the war at a displaced persons' camp at Tempelhof, Berlin. No-one would have objected to that performance. He was bringing a spot of magic into the lives of people who only weeks before had been in Belsen, Auschwitz and Dachau. From that motley assortment of humanity had come a cry from a boy: "Play 'Mein Shettele Belz'." Adler had not heard the old Yiddish folk song before and the youngster hummed it to him. Larry was delighted – so much so, that he recorded it for Decca soon after his return.

A couple of years later, Al Jolson asked him for details of the song and, as a result, it became one of my own favourite Jolson pieces, "That Wonderful Girl of Mine". In some ways, Adler's career had come full circle in 30 years. It was seeing Al Jolson perform and electrify audiences that first demonstrated to Adler what an entertainer could do. Now in a small way he was returning that experience.

Composers such as Darius Milhaud, Benjamin Britten and Vaughan Williams have written music for the mouth organ largely because of Larry Adler. Adler himself has written music for other people – most notably the theme music for that legendary picture of the early '50s, *Genevieve*. But he composes not on the mouth organ, but at the piano.

Nowhere, he says, is his work more appreciated than in Israel – the country that he said in 1962 always made him feel as though he had come home. That was not the way he put it in 1976. "It's a very spiritual feeling I have when I go there but I have never made it my home because I am a physical coward. Yet the warmth of an Israeli audience can be tremendous. It is also the most musically sophisticated audience I've ever played to.

"I remember stopping at a kibbutz and giving an impromptu concert. Kids of eight and 12 were calling for Mozart and Bach!

"I first played there in 1952. There was an enormous crowd greeting me – as though, it seemed, I was all four Beatles in one. I was being welcomed as if they were saying: 'Our Boy has come home.' "

He had first visited the country nine years earlier and had been captivated by the then Mayor of Tel Aviv, Israel Rocach. "It struck me then as a miracle that there were people in that country – it was still Palestine – who were saying: 'Send us more Jews.' "

One thing disappoints him about music in Israel. They are not making enough of their own. "It's all too derivative. The serious music is all Russian-sounding and the pop music sounds Arabic." Nevertheless, he did record "Yerushalaim Shel Zahav" (Jerusalem the Gold) and "Sharm el Sheikh", both products of the Six-Day War of 1967.

Neither, it seems, is Israel producing many violinists. "I have been told that because the violin was small and compact it became a ghetto instrument. Now, there are no ghettos in Israel and more people are learning to play the piano."

Had Larry Adler been better at the piano, he might never have become a Jewish entertainer – either on the concert platform or as he does now, giving his own one-man shows in cabaret. He might not have become a writer for serious news-papers and magazines or even contemplated the autobio-graphy he is now writing. "You know," he told me, "a journalist heard I was writing a book. He asked me what kind and I told him it would be an autobiography.

" 'Oh, yes', he said, 'of whom?' "

Joel Grey
(born 1932)

Joel Grey

Katz's Kitten

He goes on stage and says he's going to sing a country song. After all, everybody appears to be singing country songs. The orchestra tunes up for what seems like a good old country-and-western ditty, but then something strange happens. The song is very definitely in Yiddish. It is about Romania. "Well," he asks innocently. "Romania is a country isn't it?"

Thus Joel Grey makes his entrance. After three minutes, he is saying, "Eat your heart out Johnny Cash." And the audience is with him, egging him on.

Perhaps it wouldn't be wrong to call him the male Streisand. Certainly when you see Joel Grey perform – and he has taken his act from Las Vegas to the London Palladium and back to Vegas again – you know that The Generation has been reborn.

He says he is always frightened that when people come to meet him for the first time, they may have a tape measure in their pockets. The diminutive Mr. Grey, star of *Cabaret* and master of the art of the one-man show, refuses to go into details about his height. "I'll never tell," he told me.

Small he is. But it is partly that lack of height that has made him the most dynamic performer since Danny Kaye; perhaps the most individual entertainer since Jolson. "Everything about one's person affects who you are and what you are. The fact that I was the littlest person in my school class and the neighbourhood had certain disadvantages. But it also made me resourceful in certain ways that I cannot deny are positive."

He started life in 1932 as Joel Katz in Cleveland, Ohio. His father was a member of the Spike Jones crazy band – "he was

212

the one who used to go 'glug–glug' " – who then formed his own group, Mickey Katz and his Kittens. "I was one of the original kittens." Later when Dad changed his band's name to "Mickey Katz and His Kosher Jammers", Joel changed his to Joel Kaye and went on alone. "But I still get people coming up to me, asking me to sing 'Herring Boats Are a-Coming...' or the 'Geshrai of the Vilde Katchke'." The name changed again to Joel Grey and before very long he had international acclaim.

He says he loves those old comic ridiculous songs. "They were ridiculous, true, but very funny – because they were so full of funny words. Kitzel – remember Dad's song 'Tickle, Kitzel?' – Kitzel is a funny word. 'Schmaltz' is a funny word."

He doesn't sing those songs himself but he is delighted to know that Mickey Katz is still, well into the 1980s, wowing them in at that Florida geriatric home, Miami Beach. "They love him. And they don't bill him as 'Father of Joel Grey'."

In Las Vegas, which he describes as "a complete cross-section of America", they ask him to sing "Money Makes the World Go Around", from *Cabaret*, the show in which he starred with Liza Minnelli. I asked him whether he resented the fact that the film is inevitably remembered as Liza's picture.

"Not at all," he insists. "It was the Liza Minnelli, Joel Grey, Bob Fosse picture. It was a very collaborative effort. But it was the film that catapulted Liza into a kind of place in her career that was absolutely right.

"She had the media impact. But the film changed Bob Fosse's life and mine."

It was while working on the picture that Liza suggested that he go back to the live stage and do a one-man show. When he was reluctant to do so, she "in a very sneaky sort of way" made him agree to do a show with her. It was in three segments: one that Liza did alone; one that he did by himself and one with the two of them together. Only because he had the support of the girl with whom he says he still has a brother-sister relationship was he persuaded to take on something that he feared "would be as painful as it had been 15 years before, when I first did it".

To build up the act with her, he had to perfect one of his own. He tried it out at the Fairmont Hotel in San Francisco. "I was really trembling, I don't mind telling you. But it was absolutely magical, in terms of my response to it."

So to Liza Minnelli go his thanks for this new career he has made out of holding a huge cabaret or theatre audience in the palm of his hand. "She is very generous in her love for performers and the theatre."

It was in the stage version of *Cabaret* – following an American edition of *Stop the World I Want to Get Off* – that he first made a huge impact on Broadway and followed it with a show based on the life of George M. Cohan. It was called *George M*, and one of the biggest problems about this was to try to make people forget the famous James Cagney portrayal of the Broadway legend in the film *Yankee Doodle Dandy*. People who saw it said the jump from one image to the other was immediate. His regret – and mine – was that he did not have the opportunity to bring the show to London.

He continues to make films – including one recent one

playing Buffalo Bill's sidekick in a picture co-starring Paul Newman and Burt Lancaster. In another movie he plays a drug pedlar who creeps into the Sherlock Holmes legend and abducts Vanessa Redgrave. But he insists that is done "back stage .... To lift her on screen, I don't think they would hire me to do that."

He admits that he loves the stage best and says that it has a salutory effect on screen actors who have become mere celebrities. "Look what playing Broadway has done for Richard Burton. It's an immense triumph and it has legitimised his worth. He was lost in the morass of being a celebrity."

At 52 Joel Grey is happily married with two children, 24-year-old Jennifer and Jimmy, 19. "Jenny always wanted to be an actress, but I never quite believed her. Also I didn't want her to perform as a small child. I felt very strongly about that." But now he is happy for her to do so and she has helped building sets, and watched the actors and directors.

"You know, a lot of actors don't want their kids to be in the theatre. What can you be saying about yourself if you say that? The theatre is a very worthwhile place to work."

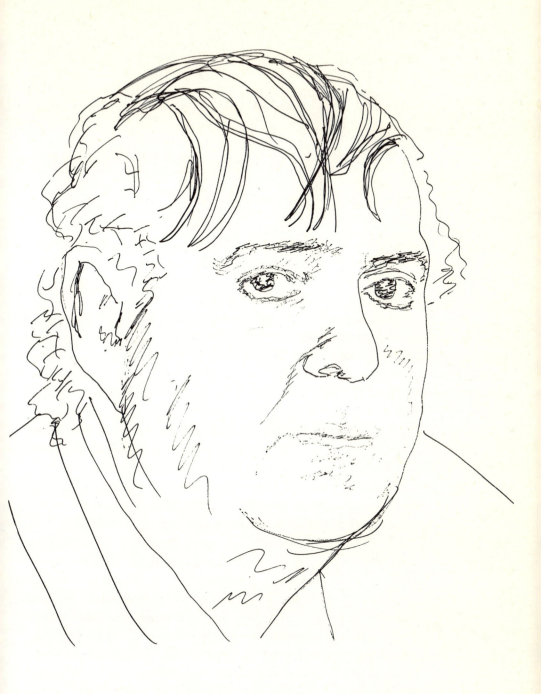

Zero Mostel
(1915–1977)

Zero Mostel

A Funny Thing Happened on the Way to Anatevka

He called himself Zero, which said nothing at all about his own opinion of his talent – other than perhaps being an outward manifestation of the inferiority complex that seemed to engulf him from time to time.

Zero Mostel was needless to say not a zero in either performance or appearance. A huge man, he superimposed himself upon any company in which he appeared. As an actor he found a series of niches from which his bulk made it difficult to escape. He was the hard-done-by con man who somehow hoped you would love him while he stole your last penny.

Even his performance as Tevya in the original Broadway production of *Fiddler on the Roof* in 1964 had the dual elements of pathos and conniving rascality that he later immortalised – a word that would not be argued over by film buffs – in *The Producers*. In *Fiddler*, it was God over whom he was trying to pull a very slight fast one.

He was not always called Zero. It was a name that stuck to him like calves' foot jelly after he failed practically every test he took at his school in Brooklyn.

Samuel Joel Mostel was born in 1915. Even if no one else believed it, he was convinced he knew more than his teachers at the grade school near his home and set out before it was too late to prove it. He was an artist who painted so well that he was encouraged to teach painting and drawing once he was awarded a place at New York's City College – from which he managed to graduate without zeros.

Become a teacher he did. Somehow, though, the days of the

Depression were not ones that promoted in him a great desire to paint.

He was a political activist as so many Jewish people of his age were when faced with the degradation of the times. Nevertheless, it was the period in history when Franklin D. Roosevelt's New Deal proclaimed the necessity of the dignity of human labour – in whatever field that may be.

Mostel had meanwhile found new outlets. He was happier singing and acting – and telling sometimes black-humour stories – than he was painting. He was also making more money at it.

He went to Hollywood and made a name for himself on Broadway. Almost always as that fat villain – casting directors had him on file for those parts. That really *was* success – in films such as *Panic in the Streets* in 1950 and *The Enforcer* a year later.

That seemed like an unbounded road to success. Until Senator McCarthy decided otherwise. You didn't come out of a Jewish neighbourhood in Brooklyn in the '30s and forget. With the rise of the UnAmerican Activities Committee, you weren't allowed to forget. Like hundreds of others, Mostel was finished.

It took until 1958 for his talent to be recognised once more. He made a series of spectacular stage appearances, first as

Leopold Bloom, in *Ulysses in Nighttown* in an off-Broadway playhouse, followed by the lead in Ionesco's *Rhinocerus* in 1961 and his biggest success to date the following year in *A Funny Thing Happened on the Way to the Forum* – which he recreated on screen in 1966. It was a major musical hit, but there was something bigger to follow the Broadway triumph, the lead in *Fiddler*.

He became the archetype Tevya, although as Topol – who starred in the role in London and later on the screen – testified, he was somewhat erratic. He could be brilliant in one performance and brittle, coarse and uncaring the next. (The two actors became firm friends – until Topol, not Zero, got the coveted film role; they later made it up.)

He also made films such as *The Angel Levine* – in which he played a poor Jewish elder who makes a pact with an enticing black devil played by Harry Belafonte; one of his most endearing performances – and *Great Catherine*.

One of his unfortunate characteristics was a desire to belittle people whom he thought he had a right to master. In the midst of a BBC interview he once gave me – in which he proceeded to talk about New York, Jews and everything but the subjects I was trying to discuss – he said: "I'm now going to eat your microphone." And did just that.

He will now probably be best remembered for his role in *The Producers* in which he played a broke Broadway "Mr. Fixit" who goes to jail by working the biggest fiddle of all time – selling shares in a show he and his partner (Gene Wilder) know just has to be an unmitigated flop. The trouble is the show is a huge success – and he has a dozen or more dear old ladies with a 60 per cent share in the operation. He was brilliant.

He died of a heart attack in 1980 while rehearsing a new interpretation of the role of Shylock in Arnold Wesker's controversial production of *The Merchant of Venice*. He doubtless would have convinced his audiences – or rather commanded them – to believe Shylock was a much more sympathetic character than Shakespeare intended.

Ron Moody
(born 1924)

Ron Moody

Reviewing the Situation

Other actors are content merely to become stars, but Ron Moody did it by reinterpreting English literature. Not only that, it could be argued that a row between Ron Moody and composer Lionel Bart deprived the anti-Semite of one of his most cherished weapons.

Moody, a graduate of the London School of Economics and practically nobody's idea of star material, had just successfully completed an audition and been chosen for the part of Fagin.

Bart and most of the other members of the team putting together the musical *Oliver* saw Fagin as everyone else had seen him – certainly as Dickens had. He was the lisping Jewish miser who cared no more for a gentile's property than he did for the welfare of the boys he had persuaded to work for him – taking a handkerchief here, a watch there.

Moody didn't see him like that. He thought he could make Fagin "kosher" without sanitising him. "For years I had hated the traditional view of Fagin, the Alec Guinness kind of miser who was such an anti-Semitic character. I thought he should be made happy, friendly, a man who told jokes and sang songs that made people laugh. Bart didn't like that at all and wouldn't speak to me for a year, but when I left the show the one who took over from me – John Bluthal – did Fagin exactly as I had done him.

"When it opened in America, it was directed in the way I did it." And, of course, when *Oliver* was filmed, Ron Moody played his old stage part in the same way that he had done in London and became an international star. Or did he? "I don't know what being a star is. I'm an actor, an artist. Why do people always expect so much from so-called stars?

"Perhaps the word artist is a bit pretentious. A painter is allowed to starve in a garret. If he wants to paint, he is allowed to paint and then tear up his work. He can choose whether he wants to do this or that or sell it if he wants to. If you're in show business you are expected to be always available and if you turn down a job, you're regarded as an idiot. A novelist is allowed some kind of freedom. So's a composer. An entertainer has to do everything that is offered to him."

He also resents having to be part businessman. "Why should I be a businessman when I employ an agent to be a businessman for me? But then again, I suppose we have to be able to protect ourselves from our agents!"

After starring in the show *Oliver*, he was offered the part on Broadway and turned it down – to demonstrate his right to starve in the garret if he wanted to, and to try to do his own "thing". Among those things was the hope that he could write and star in a show about the famous clown Grimaldi. That too, he says fell victim to his lack of freedom. The idea was taken out of his hands. Other writers took over his script, produced an inferior version of the story and the show flopped.

That memory makes him very bitter.

"I was kept waiting four years and in the end I was swallowed by a management. I got those scripts out eight years afterwards – the first two that I wrote and the third that was done by the other people and the second, the one I did, was still the best."

He did the film *Oliver* and the offers came again. Again, he turned them down.

"You have to be able to stand the pressures of success. I never could. I was surrounded by unreal people who nauseated me. I couldn't breathe properly and I wanted to get away from it. It was claustrophobic. Everyone wanted a piece of me. People want to take you over – I don't mind audiences wanting a piece of me, every performer wants that. But they wanted pieces of me outside the theatre."

The word star is so overworked, he thinks, that it no longer has any meaning. "Unless you have box office appeal and if you've got that, you don't need being called names."

The humanising of Fagin remains Moody's greatest achievement and put him on to the list of a new generation of Jewish entertainers. "We're not great any more," he says – not intending to be modest, simply to put the whole business into perspective. "There are no great entertainers any more like there used to be ... I wonder why that is?"

But he *is* very Jewish, without having to retreat into caricature constantly and without wanting to be typecast. One of his dearest wishes is to do for Shylock what he did for Fagin. He once wrote a musical version of *The Merchant of Venice* – "but nobody wanted to take a chance."

He is a man who entered the theatre comparatively late in life and has never been able to adjust to being a performer. He doesn't like actors as a breed; doesn't go drinking with them at the end of a show. "I once finished a run and then walked off when everyone else was going to a party."

He can score a fabulous success with his one-man show, have audiences cheering, critics raging and managements lining up first a West End booking and then a Broadway run – but turn it all down because it is "too hard work to do for so long". He will then add "perhaps I should have?" But you are never sure.

It is probably because Ron Moody is not like any other performer at all. While some other stars – and a star he is – race from woman to woman, from marriage to marriage, Moody has stayed a bachelor and bought his own house – which he shared with his mother and other members of his family – in the very Jewish North London suburb of Southgate. His only complaint with that life is that people are always asking him to give charity performances. "I gave a lot of them but then I found I had not time to do anything for money .... Now when I go for a walk in Southgate I'm always frightened a lady is going to stop me and say: 'Mr Moody ... I have a committee'."

He was born Ronald Moodnick in 1924, son of a sometime

grocer and set builder at Elstree Studios. That way, he is a second-generation native Briton. His paternal grandparents came over from Russia. His mother was born in Vilna, once the centre of Jewish learning. "I'm very proud of that Russian background," he told me.

It was at the age of five that he was first smitten by the theatre bug. "I was a natural mimic. I used to imitate everybody I knew. When I went to the pictures I'd come back all starry-eyed and imitate what I had just seen. Hollywood was a Mecca, a place I'd never ever get to. I wonder what sort of dream factory the kids have today? They surely can't get the same fun out of pop singers?

"It was wonderful going to a film and sitting through the whole programme twice and three times. I've seen some of those films I used to rave about as a kid and they're terrible now."

He was brought up on *Lives of a Bengal Lancer, Gone With the Wind* and anything with Charles Laughton. His real inspiration was the Marx Brothers – with Buster Keaton, and Laurel and Hardy thrown in.

The Marx Brothers stand out – "perhaps it was their anarchy that I liked. I can't bear restrictions. I can't bear to think that an audience isn't there."

Without that audience he is not just lost, he is intensely shy.

He discovered at the London School of Economics that he could lose the shell-like prison that being shy created for him. At the L.S.E. he put on a Groucho Marx moustache and so made a mask behind which he could hide.

"I was so shy I couldn't even speak up in class. All the other students would speak and use long words that no one knew. I would just sit there nodding, pretending I understood everything. There were lots of things I wanted to say, but never did.

"I was refectory officer in the students union. I didn't speak once in my whole year of office. On my last day in the union somebody thought he'd have a go at me and deliberately asked a question. So I stood up and said in a Welsh accent: 'I shouldn't be at all surprised, actually,' and sat down. At least, I went out on a laugh."

But he performed in school concerts, and Groucho's moustache carried him into a new world. "Instead of being shy, I suddenly became the greatest verbaliser of the lot. Suddenly I *was* Groucho. I was speaking, I was talking. It was like the opening of a dam. There was this tremendous freedom I'd never known before. It wasn't me being judged, it was another person. I had no reason to be nervous."

Yet, all the time he was studying, he remained stage struck. He studied sociology and obtained a degree in the subject — but he was secretly buying copies of *The Stage*.

"I just didn't want to tell anybody. I'd walk up and down outside the newsagent before I'd buy a copy. It was as though by buying the paper in public I was revealing a dreadful secret. It was like going into a chemist and buying a packet of contraceptives, which I still don't like doing. There was a kind of shame in doing something that was perfectly reasonable, quite all right, but I didn't have the guts to go and do it. When I got my first role at Elstree Studios, it was in the accounts department."

He took up sociology because he was a dedicated socialist — "dreadfully concerned about the world and wanting to reform society. It is still a strong part of my attitude to life, but I've done nothing about it. I feel quite a failure in that regard."

Reading George Bernard Shaw in the R.A.F. made a big impact on him. "I thought that before I got involved in anything serious I should learn about people and I thought that the only way to learn about people was taking this sociology course."

The real reason he studied sociology he now admits is that he wanted to be another Shaw and thought it would help him with his writing as much as he says it did with his performing. "I wanted to be a messiah, to change the world. I am sure that is deeply-rooted in all Jewish people.

"One of the three tenets of Judaism is the giving of charity. Doing good is an essential part of our life.

226

"I became more and more involved in the stage and the two things went hand in hand. In fact, the sociology became invaluable."

He made no definite decision to leave the L.S.E. In fact, he was still following an M.Sc. course in sociology while struggling against the hardest audience ever for a male entertainer – that at the Windmill. He had to fill in the moments when the nude and near-nude girls were taking a rest – and thereby obliged to watch the "steeplechase" of men jumping from one row to another in order to get a closer glance at an expanse of naked female flesh when the demented comedian had at last shut his mouth.

He himself has often wondered about the success ratio of Jewish entertainers – "a group who just have to entertain without thinking about why. There is some kind of insecurity about it. They have to find a way of getting round it. The way they choose is to make people laugh. They hear applause and it's their ticket to acceptability. Rather like some kids who become footballers. If they didn't do that, they'd be on the streets beating up people."

If Moody hadn't been as shy, "inadequate and uncertain" as he was at the time he left school, he would have become a teacher. "I was for a few weeks, but I was no good at it. They could smell me out. I'd be all right now. I'd know how to be boss."

Now he says he doesn't question himself. "I know what I'm good at, so I only want to do the things that I am good at. I went to see Sir Laurence Olivier in a play once and he was bad in it. He should never have done it."

He likes to think about his Jewish roots and always the conversation switches to Fagin. In America he once attended a communal seder – the first evening of Passover when the story of the Exodus of the Children of Israel from Egypt is recited by Jews the world over. An elderly woman stared him in the face and said: "Why did you do this Fagin? You gave us a black eye!" "I said 'If it has to be done at all, isn't it better that a Jew should do it than someone else?' I presumed to change

227

literature. I think it was one of the most constructive things I ever did."

The producers of the show wanted to make Fagin a cockney. He insisted on Fagin remaining a Jew – but a lovable one. He describes his year in the show as "12 months of misery. I just couldn't stand the company any more – that's why I wouldn't do it on Broadway. I was always a very dedicated ruthless performer. It was killing once I got on that stage."

One of the reasons for Ron Moody's elusive approach to stardom is that he will not abandon being a writer for a role on stage. He has to write as well as perform; unless he can do that, there seems to be something lacking in anything he does.

Three times he played Captain Hook in J.M. Barrie's play for children, *Peter Pan*. He considered it so "twee" that he was depressed at the idea of taking on the dual role of the pirate captain and Mr Darling, father of Peter Pan's friend Wendy. The only way he could do so was to almost obliterate the original conception of the role with his own "business" and by ad-libbing. "I'm very much an anarchist at heart and I think the anarchy ran riot in that show. I took some real liberties but it seemed to go over."

It went over so well, in fact, that the part was his for life – had he wanted it. Being Ron Moody, of course, he didn't.

Before *Oliver* he was in revue – "and I had to get a laugh a second. Otherwise, I couldn't stand it."

He didn't want to be typecast but Fagin led to a flood of Jewish role offers. The only Jewish roles he was happy to accept were in television plays – as a man dying in a Catholic hospital, and as an ageing boxing promoter.

There's a feeling of bitterness inside Ron Moody – mostly at the way managements have treated him in England, a country he regards "as just death".

He is frightened of being "in an unfinished state without any real polish. In the one-man show I did, I really felt that I broke through. I didn't get stale because I changed it every night."

But it was too hard work to do on Broadway or in the West End. "I used to work during the first half, slop out during the interval, change and then go through it again." Being on stage is, he says, "my seat of power. Sometimes I've been given so much power that I get frightened and pull myself back."

In Hollywood he played a Jewish-type role in a film called *The Twelve Chairs*. "I was very proud of that, but it was completely ignored. Nobody reviewed it."

The film he isn't proud of was a horror picture – *Legend of the Werewolf*. "I was ashamed of that. I did it for money because it was a bad year. The critics reviewed that and slated it. They were right. I was bad."

He was never more conscious of power than when he did cabaret. Churchills, the Coconut Grove, supper clubs such as the Jack of Clubs. "Stickiest places in the world. But you can really have power there."

For a time he was constantly plagued with requests to do Jewish acts. Then, quite suddenly the word was spread that they weren't fashionable anymore. "Suddenly Jewish people became ashamed of their origins. They didn't want to be reminded of them. They didn't like heimishe jokes. If you started talking with an accent, they didn't like it. They wanted to be considered English.

"My theory is that that's the reason for the Jews' pre-occupation with Israel. It's an attempt to get rid of the guilt they feel for having abandoned their Jewishness. They make up for their own conscience by putting everything into raising money for Israel."

He has never been to Israel himself but he says he feels "so bloody proud of some of the things they do. It really makes you want to *qvell*.

"There's something dashing — swashbuckling — romantic about the things they've done."

He considers himself a religious person, although not strictly Orthodox. But he will never eat pork, bacon or ham. "I often wonder why the Israelis fight Arabs. Neither of them eat pigmeat, do they?"

In 1981 while working in Hollywood in a TV series in which he played a Scotland Yard cop on loan to the American police he fell in love and became engaged to a non-Jewish girl.

"She taught me to go back to my religion. With her I went to shul every shabbos. We broke up and I came back to London but I still go to shul. I love it."

Ron Moody must rank as one of a new generation of outstanding Jewish entertainers. But a very frustrated one. "I wanted to be part of the British musical. *Oliver* was a start, but after that nothing. They'll take what I write myself, but no one comes to me with any offers. I was offered the Talk of the Town," he recalls, referring to the London nightspot, "but that was taken back because they thought there were going to be too many foreigners in the audience." So he went back to America — and then turned down half a million dollars because he couldn't face doing Fagin again. (In the winter of 1983–4, he succumbed to a limited London season in the role.) He worked in television in Los Angeles, but after two years decided he hated California and came back to Southgate.

He wrote two acclaimed novels, and thought it was easier to write books than to act. But, really, he still wanted to do both. And, above all, to write for the stage.

"I've done two shows and had them turned down. I'm going to write my third under a pseudonym."

230

Mel Brooks
(born 1926)

Mel Brooks

Blazing Borsht

Mel Brooks – or as his birth certificate states, Melvin Kaminsky; as far as one can gather, no relation of that other Kaminsky who became Danny Kaye – is a throwback. Like the younger Woody Allen, he is the old Jewish comedian in a new mould.

He's not quite the wunderkind that Allen turned out to be. He was born in a New York East Side tenement – would he have achieved quite so much had he not been? – in 1926, early enough to have worked in the Borsht belt where he entertained extravagantly-fed New York Jews with the kind of jokes they believed were divinely inspired for their hearing.

Sometimes it was just using a string of Yiddish words told in the Bronx dialect.

He was at one hotel the day a maid was stuck for 12 hours in a linen cupboard. He began his act by quoting the words that were heard by her rescuer and which, with considerable laughter, were being retold by every guest in the dining room. "Loz mir arois." (Let me out.) "Loz mir arois." The hotel collapsed in laughter.

He enjoyed recalling the time that one hotel executive was heard on the public address system as he bewailed the standards of his paying customers.

"Filty rotten! How can they leave a sheet so filty?"

It was enough. The people laughed.

They booked to come to the resort hotels again – killing themselves in the process with a diet that sent their doctors into fits of apoplexy – and young Mr Kaminsky was set on a career in show business.

Actually, it had started earlier. When he had attended the

232

Sussex Camp for Underprivileged Children, he found himself the centre of attraction. "I always felt it was my job to amuse those around me." They considered themselves amused – and he more than enjoyed obliging.

He even learned to play the drums – and his first serious entertainment job was working in a jazz band.

During World War Two, he served in the American Army and actually learned to ride a horse. "Imagine that! A Jewish kid on a horse!"

Maurice Yacowar in his book *The Comic Art of Mel Brooks* quotes the remarks that some people have been tasteless enough to make about Brooks's lack of affection for the Germans. Brooks replies: "Me? Not like the Germans? Why should I not like the Germans? Just because they're arrogant and have fat necks and do anything they're told so long as it's cruel and killed millions of Jews in concentration camps and made soap out of their bodies and lamp shades out of their skins. Is that any reason to hate their f---ing guts?

"A Jew always walks bent," he says – "just in case there's trouble."

When the war was over, after a spell working in a shirt factory, he served his apprenticeship in television – in that veritable nursery of comic TV personalities (and so graphically portrayed in Richard Benjamin's movie *My Favourite Year*) the Sid Caesar Show.

When you work on an organisation like that, you do one of two things – you stay or you decide you could do just as well working for yourself.

He decided to go it alone, or rather on his own behalf, teaming up with another brilliant comic writer cum performer Carl Reiner. In 1960, the two of them produced an LP album which has become a comedy classic, "The 2,000-Year-Old Man" – the man newly discovered by a radio interviewer who has seen it all.

"Did you know Joan of Arc?" the interviewer asks.

"Know her," says the man, "know her. I went with her, dummy."

He created other characters – including Dr Akiba, the Israeli heart specialist. "Where do you practise?" the doctor is asked.

"Practise?" he recoils in horror. "I don't have to practise. I'm good at it."

Indeed he is.

His first huge film success was *The Producers* in which Zero Mostel and Gene Wilder think they have found the way out of insolvency by producing a Broadway flop. It includes the magnificent epitome of bad taste, the production number called "Springtime for Hitler and Germany". It was a brilliant idea – selling 60 per cent of the show here, 50 there, another 40 here. Since there was no question that the show would flop, all the producers needed to worry about was dividing the surplus percentages among themselves. It went wrong – because the show was a smash hit – and how many 60 per cents of the profits for "angels" can there be? It takes a mind like Brooks's to work that one out.

The Twelve Chairs with Ron Moody going behind the Iron Curtain came next and Brooks himself had a part. It whetted his appetite for more. In the hilarious *Blazing Saddles* of 1974, he is both the Governor and the Indian Chief – with the legend Kosher for Pesach in Hebrew characters on his head-dress.

Young Frankenstein – featuring the late English-born comedian Marty Feldman – *Silent Movie* (a bizarre attempt at recapturing the past if ever there was one, this), and *History of the World Part One* followed as quickly as he could put the ideas down onto paper.

And there was one distinct departure from the Brooks style and workload. He produced the film, *The Elephant Man* about the misshapen, pathetic man found in a circus by a doctor at the London Hospital. He didn't write or act in the film himself, but he contributed greatly to the art and usefulness of the cinema by making it available.

However, neither he nor his public would want him to be remembered for that. At times he could claim to *be* American comedy – and Jewish comedy in particular. No mean achievement.

"I'll never do a serious picture just to make a profound statement," he says. "I can make those statements comically. You don't have to stop laughing."

And fortunately, people haven't. Perhaps because he says what a lot of other people think. He certainly says what a lot of his (Jewish) contemporaries think.

"When I was a little boy, I thought when I grew up, I would talk Yiddish, too. I thought little kids talked English, but when they grew up they would talk Yiddish like the adults did. There would be no reason to talk English anymore, because we would have made it."

Melvin Kaminsky made it. Maybe that's why he still speaks Yiddish.

George Jessel
(1898–1981)

George Jessel

Toastmaster General

In America he is still remembered as the nation's Toastmaster General. When it came to the funeral of a top show business personality just occasionally he would not be found delivering the eulogy. At one time he was seen very much more often on such occasions – but they started drying up. The Generation were nearly all gone. Before he himself died in 1981 almost all of them had had George Jessel see them on their way with a turn of poetic phrase written without the aid of a scriptwriter. He was a clever man, but not clever enough to find a way to deliver his own funeral oration.

Young people never knew him so well, which is a pity. In almost any story of his contemporaries Jessel was something of a lynchpin. The man who was there. The one who knew the big stars, who cheered with them at their triumphs, wept with them with their turkeys and usually found the time to kiss them on the cheek – his favourite way of showing his affection. He did it to presidents, to generals, to superstars and to girls. Always to girls.

He bathed so much in other people's glories that his own talents as a comic were perhaps never displayed to the full. As an example, he was constantly mentioning the man who to him was not only the World's Greatest Entertainer, but also the Biggest Son of a Bitch of them all – Al Jolson.

It was Jolson who beat him to the coveted role in *The Jazz Singer* and so prevented him from becoming the first big star of sound movies. But as he readily conceded: "he was better than I was."

Jessel had started off in 1908 as a ten-year-old playing with Eddie Cantor in *Kid Kabaret*. At the time of his barmitzvah he suggested that his mother buy him a suit that would also do for his wedding. He was only partly kidding – he was already sexually experienced. He was very soon also experienced in the world of the theatre, soaking up everything he could about the people he admired most.

From vaudeville, he went to straight drama – achieving national recognition and stardom with the part of the cantor's son in the Broadway production of Sampson Raphael's play *The Jazz Singer*, originally called *The Day of Atonement*. The play was a sell-out, and people say that it could have gone on forever. What prevented that was Warner Brothers and a deal they made with Al Jolson. When the film company bought the rights of *The Jazz Singer*, it was taken for granted that Jessel was going to star in it. But Warners were going broke and needed a gimmick that overnight could take them out of the red. They found it in Vitaphone, a process for recording film soundtrack on disc.

The story is that Jessel was not happy risking his career on the new invention. Certainly Eddie Cantor did not want to, but Jolson took the plunge and the rest is history. Jessel himself tells it slightly differently. He says that he was staying in the same hotel in New York with Jolson one weekend when Al decided to go out alone for a walk. He didn't say where he was going. "The next morning I read in the papers that Al had signed to make *The Jazz Singer*. Is it any wonder I always felt bitter? I felt sick. It was my part and partly my story. Jolson got the role because he put money into it."

George did, however, himself make films. His most famous was *Lucky Boys* – trading very much on the reputation of *The Jazz Singer*, and the later *Singing Fool* – in which he sang the maudlin "My Mother's Eyes", doing what appeared to be a Jolson imitation – something he did frequently (one of the last occasions being a memorial meeting for his old antagonist).

Sam Goldwyn once said: "If Lincoln had ever heard Jessel sing, he'd have shot him first."

Unlike the other members of The Generation, George Jessel had roots that were almost aristocratic. His namesake and second cousin of his father had been Sir George Jessel, Solicitor General and then Master of the Rolls in Britain.

His own grandfather Edward Aaron Jessel came to America in 1835, joined the gold rush and later became a Chicago auctioneer. His father was a playwright of sorts and then a travelling salesman.

George Jessel was born in New York in 1898 – a city he was later to describe as a "sewer", and worse. But when he grew up it was a place of magic, where showpeople were kings and princes to a youngster who thought that the gates to heaven had a box office and paradise a proscenium arch.

As the years went by, he became a sought-after vaudeville comedian, going from place to place. Later on, he discovered a new talent – making speeches. He became part of the Jimmy Walker circle, the group who helped make James J. Walker, Mayor of New York. Walker – "Beau James" as he was known – was an Irish-American who had as many Italians and Jews as friends and enemies as anyone who ever lived in that most cosmopolitan of cities. A brilliant lawyer, he used to prefer writing songs to winning cases – one of these "Will You Love Me in December as You Do in May" became a hit – and he loved being with girls better than solving the problems of Manhattan's streets. He was eventually sacked for corruption. But Jessel was as much responsible for putting him in power as any of the Tammany Hall big shots. He made almost 500 speeches for him – a feat he would repeat for a dozen mayors and half as many presidents.

Sometimes his speeches were not quite the epitome of tact he thought they were.

In July 1941, before America had entered World War Two, Jessel made a speech on behalf of Chinese relief at Lum Fon's restaurant on 52nd Street, New York.

"When I was a boy", he said, "the only Chinese I knew were the peace-loving men who always conducted themselves with dignity. They would deliver up our laundry only when we had the tickee to give them. And so it is today. All China has the laundry America needs – the will to combat fascist aggression

240

before it sweeps to the Pacific. Yes, they have the laundry. So let's give them the tickee." He then passed the hat around.

Girls were always Jessel's weakness. Sometimes he married them. Sometimes he did not. One of his most famous wives was Norma Talmadge, an actress who seems to have been as much under his spell as he was under hers.

He became an impresario and theatrical producer – but never missing the opportunity to play himself whenever possible. From Broadway he went to Hollywood, producing such memorable films as *Dancing in the Dark* and *When My Baby Smiles At Me*, in which he introduced Dan Dailey and Betty Grable – and dozens that were not.

Jessel always took pride in his discoveries. He liked to call George Burns "my theatrical godson". It was he who persuaded Burns to do on stage what he always did so successfully off it – mesmerise people with his wit. As he said once: "Offstage (Burns) had the confidence of General George Patton, Sophie Tucker and the New York Giants."

Jessel became a household name with a radio act – in which he would make imaginary telephone calls to his mother. "Hello Mama ..." he would say and go on to listen to the troubles of a Yiddisher Mama who was very different from his own aristocratic parent. He stopped them when she died in 1945. When audiences asked him to carry on he said in a typical lachrymose phrase: "You can't get heaven on the phone." They loved that in 1945.

He also made a film with Anthony Newley and Joan Collins called *Can Heironymus Merkin Ever Forget Mercy Hummpe and Find True Happiness?* No one found any happiness at all from that film –least of all Jessel, although he must have made a dollar or two from it and was surrounded by lots of nude girls. Perhaps he didn't like being called Dr. Death. He has also had a small part in an Orson Welles film that has yet to find an exhibitor.

The wars in Korea and Vietnam gave Jessel a chance to show his talent at the microphone to the full and by all accounts the troops loved every hammy moment of it. The

241

trips to the war zones – never very far from the sound of gunfire – gave him a chance to indulge himself in one of his favourite pastimes, dressing up in uniforms of one kind or another. He used to enjoy appearing on television in them, but there were not a great many of those occasions since he had a bust-up with TV host Edwin Newman on the NBC "Today" show. Exception was taken to his describing the *New York Times* as another *Pravda*.

He was always an ardent supporter of Jewish causes. He was one of the founders of the Jewish Theatrical League and probably raised more money for Israel than any other single American. Much of the after-dinner speaking for which he earned his title of Toastmaster General was for Israel. With one eye constantly watering, he could bring more emotion from an after-dinner speech than anyone who ever stood before a microphone.

Pictures of him with David Ben Gurion (kissing him) and with Abba Eban (shaking hands) rub shoulders in his collection of photographs with Queen Elizabeth II (at a command performance), and with Presidents Harry Truman (kissing him), John F. Kennedy, Lyndon B. Johnson and Richard Nixon – about whose "crucifixion" he intended to write a book.

He was also the author of six books about himself. Every one of them a history of Broadway.

Frankie Vaughan
(born 1928)

Frankie Vaughan

Behind the Green Door

Frank Ableson did his first singing in a synagogue choir. Heard that one before? He came from a poor family. So tell me something new! He was virtually brought up by his grandmother. Yes – and so was Eddie Cantor. He later changed his name … Enough already! From such a story you expect people to be interested?

Well, perhaps the bare facts *are* against him. They seemed to feature in every story that came out of New York's East Side and ended up on Broadway. But wait, there is a difference. Frank Ableson was born in Liverpool, grew up in Leeds and became an international singing star, living in London. And the name he took was Frankie Vaughan.

Singing came to Frankie early – but nobody in the family had ever done it seriously and that was the last thing his parents expected him to do. Not that they had a great deal of time to think about anything. "I was born to good parents," Frankie now insists, but most of their efforts were confined to trying to scrape a living – his father as an upholsterer, his mother as a seamstress. So it was with his grandmother that he was left most of the time. She was born in Kiev and came to Britain when she was deserted by her husband, a soldier in the Russian Army.

Because Frankie spent so much time with his grandmother, she was the real influence on his early life – but more of that soon. For the moment, think of a youngster whose first singing was at the Hebrew School in Liverpool. "I used to sing at home for parties too – but the only way I would do it was with the light out or behind the curtain or in another room," he recalls today. "I was very shy. And I still am, for that matter."

244

So there were no theatrical ambitions in those days. But singing did become more and more important to him — particularly when at the age of ten he first joined that synagogue choir. He sang in a strong alto voice that no one could ever confuse with a girl's. And his fame spread beyond the synagogue and, indeed, beyond the local Jewish community. When the kids of the neighbourhood had to take refuge in the air-raid shelters, it was Frankie who was always asked to entertain with the latest pop songs. "I'd only do it if every single light in the air raid shelter was switched off. Then, in complete darkness, I'd get up and sing 'I Don't Want to Set the World on Fire'." He didn't have that problem in the synagogue. The boy choristers were always hidden from the rest of the congregation in a special choir loft.

Frankie was the second of his parents' children. He had an elder sister, Myra. Then, during the war, came a second sister, Carol. His father was by then a sergeant major in the Pioneer Corps.

Now Mr. Ableson, Senior, had moved from Liverpool, taking his family first to a village in Westmorland which had probably never seen a Jewish face before, and then on to Lancaster, which to this day has still not seen many. At Lancaster, Frank Ableson was enrolled at the Boys' National School. "I was just over 13 and I was belligerent. Really I was a bit of a tearaway."

It was at that school that Frankie discovered a latent talent — as an artist. He also joined the Lancaster Lads Club and learned to box. For a long time it was a toss-up as to whether he became a commercial artist or a boxer. Being a singer still didn't come into it, although while at the Lancaster College of Art — he had won a scholarship there at 14½, 18 months earlier than most of the other students — he sang in the dance band and took part in rags. In those days his idols were Al Jolson, Eddie Cantor and Sophie Tucker. Perhaps you've heard that before, too.

By the time that he joined the Royal Army Medical Corps — and became an Army boxing champion — he thought he was going to teach art as a career. And when he became engaged to the girl whom he had met at the Locarno ballroom in Leeds, he was already a student teacher at the Leeds College of Art.

His fiancée was Stella Shock, a friend of his sister Myra and a young lady who he didn't think could be very nice – or she wouldn't have gone to the Locarno unescorted. He changed his mind about that very soon. As he did about his singing.

In London on the proceeds of the prize won in a competition to design a furniture exhibition stand, he auditioned for Hughie Green's radio version of "Opportunity Knocks". He couldn't get on to the show as a single, so teamed up with a girl singer called Irene Griffin. They came second. Then he met an agent called Billy Marsh, got himself a week at the Kingston Empire – and was an instant hit with the audience.

"Billy told me," Frankie says today, "I think you're in showbusiness." It was the veteran entertainer Hetty King who pulled him down to size. "Yes," she said, "You have a place in show business, young man. But you've got to learn your trade."

One of the first things he did learn about that trade was that the name Ableson didn't go down too well. It would today, but in the early 1950s, the kindest thing that could be said about it was that it wasn't, shall we say, very commercial. He and Marsh went looking for substitutes. "What was your mother's maiden name?" Marsh asked. "Kozak," Frankie replied. "Kozak," said Marsh. "No. That's no good." He didn't know that a TV detective was going to do well enough with a name that was remarkably similar.

The search went on. Finally, Frankie's grandmother told his mother: "Tell him that whatever he calls himself, he is still my number-vorn grandson." When the youngster heard about this, he chuckled appreciatively and told Billy Marsh about it.

"I'm still her number-vorn grandson," repeated Frankie. "That's a good name," said Marsh. "Vaughan. Frankie Vaughan." And so that's what he became. And in many people's eyes he was the number-vorn singer who learned to recognise a good song when he heard one and to develop a

246

style that is uniquely his own. Not everyone likes the idea of a singer who giggles, throws out a leg and sticks a top hat at a rakish angle on his head, but there are hundreds of thousands who do.

His first big break was at the Hulme Hippodrome in Manchester where, soon after the name change, he earned £100 a week, topping the bill. Success didn't last that long. When he married Stella in 1951, their first London home was above a transport café behind Kings Cross station. Then, in 1954, he made his first recording on the HMV label, a song called "My Sweetie Went Away". He sang with the Ken Mackintosh Band and it did well enough for it to be followed by "No Help Wanted" and "Look at that Girl". And then came the big break. He met Val Parnell, head of the London Palladium and of the vast Moss Empire circuit – or at least it was still vast in 1954. Frankie went on a tour of the circuit and his name became known around the country.

In a Glasgow music shop he discovered an old piece of sheet music, entitled "Give Me the Moonlight". The rest, as they say, is history. It became identified with him and took Frankie Vaughan around the world, collecting bigger audiences and louder applause wherever he went. Songs like "The Green Door", "Loop De Loop" followed and later on there were his own characteristic versions of "Cabaret", "Mame" and "Hello Dolly".

In 1960, he went to Hollywood to make the film *Let's Make Love* with Marilyn Monroe. It was not a great success, but Frankie's main problem was that he didn't like being away from home. He couldn't return to England and the family quickly enough. A little later on, the same reason forced him to give up the chance of starring in his own Broadway show playing one of the giants of The Generation, Harry Richman.

He contented himself with SRO (standing room only) audiences at London's Talk of the Town, in Australia and in a dozen other countries – but always where he knew he would be away for just a limited time.

In Britain, he was able to exercise his passion for helping

boys' clubs. "I consider that England has been very good to me and very good to the Jewish people," he told me. "I decided that my way of showing my appreciation was by helping in the boys' clubs." It was valued help, Frankie was chosen to sit on a commission looking into the problems of juvenile delinquency and a few years later was awarded the OBE for his efforts.

"I looked upon it as a gesture which gave a dignity to my profession," he said about that. "I was the first pop singer to be given the OBE."

But his proudest success has been his family. He and Stella are very close – as they are to their three children.

He admits there is something peculiarly, specially Jewish about the closeness of the Vaughan family – who go to synagogue together on the High Festivals, a time when he never works. Occasionally, he and his sons also go there on the Sabbath. His one unfulfilled ambition is to conduct a synagogue service – "but I don't know enough yet to do it."

Recently he went to Israel as an ordinary member of a tourist group, calling himself Frankie Ableson. Other people on the coach asked him to sing, but he said he didn't want to be thought to be showing off. He made up for it on his return to Britain, by recording a distinctive version of "Hava Nagela". He is an ardent Zionist – but that did not prevent him from being in a party of artists at a Command Performance show in London attended by King Hussein of Jordan.

He says he's lucky. "Lucky to have a talent and to have my health. Lucky to have met such a wonderful girl as my wife Stella. Lucky to have such a wonderful family. Lucky to have healthy kids. And a job I adore."

Bob Dylan
(born 1941)

Bob Dylan

Blowin' in the Wind

When Bob Dylan announced that he was a born-again Christian, a section of America's Jewish community was prepared to take out the low stools and "sit shiva" – the seven-day mourning period following the death of a loved one. The practice used to be regularly adopted following the decision of a Jew to marry outside the faith.

Dylan was seen to do worse than that. He embraced another faith and did it in public. He sang songs about it. He told how he saw Jesus in a vision.

Four years later, he was photographed at the Western Wall in Jerusalem, a *tallet* (prayer shawl) wrapped around him, *tephillin* (phylacteries) entwined on his arm and in place on his forehead. It was his son's barmitzvah and both of them had come home.

The rock generation had, in the meantime, gained respectability and Dylan the sometime High Priest of the Flower People had been seen to mature. When the friends of the Zimmerman family in Duluth, Minnesota, a town which freezes for half the year and swelters in the height of the summer, heard the news that he was also studying at an Orthodox *yeshivah* (talmudical college) in the Israeli capital, they felt free once more to cheer the success of the local boy made good. (For years the local rabbi had been known to carry a picture in his wallet of the singer, dressed, it seemed like a Chassid – it was just the way he liked to appear while "doing his own thing" – and use it as a talisman to bring in new members).

Such is the role of the Jewish entertainer. Bob Dylan's own role was, however, much more that of singer to the masses –

250

and a total contradiction everywhere you turned. He was supposedly a folk singer, yet the songs he sang were those of named composers – usually himself. He sang rock tunes that were seen to have a spiritual content long before he told the world he had been born again.

He preached love and peace, yet was reputed to be a member of the extremist Jewish Defence League.

Dylan knew he was worrying people – and he worried too.

He brought it all on himself, of course. He claimed to have seen visions in his childhood. When interviewers wanted to talk to him about the role of religion in music, he countered by saying: "Why doesn't anyone ever ask Kris Kristofferson questions like that?"

He was born in Duluth in 1941 and began singing and writing songs at the age of 12. He was first noticed by the rock generation after moving to New York in his teens. He admitted from the start that he was influenced by other people – such as Joan Baez, with whom he later acted and directed in a film, and by an Egyptian singer called Om Kalthoum, whom he heard first in Jerusalem. He liked the Beatles, too and when John Lennon wrote his first book, he was asked to write one, too. It was in some ways merely a further requirement before an entertainer could be regarded as a total success in the 1960s.

What he really became well known for were the songs that were always to be identified with him, songs that he would maintain said as much to him as to the people listening to them. "Lay, Lady, Lay" (which had been commissioned for *Midnight Cowboy*), "Like a Rolling Stone" and "Blowin' in the Wind" helped earn him the title of poet as well as singer.

Like most poets, however, the sadness all too often seemed to overwhelm the joy – even at Woodstock, that paradise of the rock hungry, where there was a blur of faces for as far as the eye could see when Dylan entertained, and when a British open-air concert could attract 150,000.

These were, however, sufficiently impressive credentials for journalists to hang on every word he uttered. And always about his faith. "I'm interested in what and who a Jew is", he declared on one occasion. "I'm interested in the fact that Jews are Semites like Babylonians, Hittites, Arabs, Syrians and Ethiopians. But a Jew is different because a lot of people hate Jews. There's something going on here that is hard to explain."

Years later, after he had abandoned his Judaism and then returned to it, he said: "My roots are in Egypt. They went down there with Joseph, and they came back out with Moses, you know the guy that killed the Egyptian, married an Ethiopian girl and brought the law down from the mountain ... I can tell you that much, but it's sleepy time down south."

Now, as Jack L. Warner would say, uneasy lies the head that wears the toilet seat – and being sleepy time down south doesn't necessarily make it any clearer. But the former Robert Zimmerman thought he knew what he was saying, a disease that a number of people could claim was caught by too many pop singers who saw themselves as soothsayers to the nation.

He is, nevertheless, quite clearly an exceptionally intelligent man who has seen his career wax and wane like that of many another entertainer – and perhaps in direct proportion to his attachment to Judaism. Also, like other entertainers, he has been tempted to give less than his best in return for promised riches. A London "quality" paper critic described one Dylan album as "the most embarrassing piece of plastic ever produced in the name of a great artist."

The fact that he was described by such a journal as "a great artist" was enough to lift him far above the ranks of mere pop singers. Others, meanwhile, have always regarded him as a crusader to be valued. His outspoken comments against the bomb and against the Vietnam war undoubtedly influenced a generation – and they, in turn, influenced those who had been born both long before and after them. He knew that and he exploited it.

But he would still say: "What people think or say about me doesn't affect me." On the contrary, it affected him very deeply indeed.

He would sing "Times They Are a Changin'", but while there were people ready to pay good money to attend his concerts, it was enough. "The starving artist is a myth", he told one journalist. "Who says an artist can't have any money? Look at Picasso. You don't have to starve to be a good artist. Look at Matisse, he was a banker."

Writers complained that he spoke in monosyllables. Sometimes he also spoke in poetry. "Have you ever lain with someone when your hearts were beating in the same rhythm? That's true love."

He fought racism – not anti-Semitism particularly. He was much more concerned with civil rights for the blacks. He said he hated war – and focused the blame on the world's toy makers who made model guns. "They are as much to be held responsible for death and destruction of the planet as any important arms manufacturer. They're just doing it for little people. They're the ones that start the assembly line of death."

It sounded nicer to the accompaniment of his guitar and expressed thus:

> *How many years can a mountain exist*
> *Before it's washed to the sea?*
> *Yes 'n' how many times can some people exist*
> *Before they're allowed to be free?*

The answer we were told was "blowin' in the wind". But many of the people who paid to hear him believed it was coming from the loudspeakers in front of them. The man who had eschewed one religion, found another, and then returned to his first developed into a cult figure.

Audiences listened to his brand of political-Nashville-black music, studied the words that he sang from platforms in the Deep South of the States and on the Isle of Wight and were convinced his was a message to take away.

But he always insisted that he didn't write political songs. "Political songs are slogans. I don't even know the definition

253

of politics. At one time, it could have been a good thing, but right now, it's all part of that so-called corruptible clown. Like, you know, the law is a good thing until it's used against the innocent."

But there *is* another side to Dylan — unlike so many other stars of his generation he has a certain inbuilt modesty. He was once asked by the *New Musical Express* newspaper if he was satisfied with most of the records he made.

"No, no, no. It's unbearable to hear some of them .... I want to shut them off. The sound of my voice, I can't get used to it. Never have gotten used to it. Makes you wanna hide ... (but) I like all my records when I make them."

What is not so unusual is the equally inbuilt doubt and insecurity — which some might see as the root of all his religious trouble. In a book he wrote called *Tarantula* he penned for himself an epitaph that began, "Here lies Bob Dylan. Murdered. From behind. By trembling flesh." Later he told a journalist: "Those were in my wild unnatural moments. I'm glad those feelings passed."

Those feelings, his psychologist might decide could have come from his youth in Minnesota. Certainly it was from there that he first picked the sounds that later became his songs. Or the lack of sound, as he explained: "In the city there is nowhere you can go where you don't hear sound. You are never alone. I don't think I could have done it [in New York]. Just the struggle of growing up would be immense and would really distort things if you wanted to be an artist .... A lot of creative people come out of New York but I don't know anyone like myself. I meet a lot of people from New York that I get along with fine and share the same ideas, but I've got something different in my soul. ... it is like being from the Smokey Mountains or the backwoods of Mississippi. It is going to make you a certain type of person If you stay twenty years in one place."

Staying put is something Bob Dylan has never done.

Dylan, some people have said, has spent too much of his

time talking about religion. But, then, unlike most other show people, he sees much of his work as a spiritual crusade, a session in front of the microphone an experience others only get in church or synagogue.

"There's a mystic in all of us. It's part of our nature," he explains. That was why, after a serious motorcycle accident, he chose to make what he calls "the first Biblical rock album," based on stories from the Bible. And then, in a sentence that could easily form part of a Dylan lyric, adds: "I can see God in a daisy. I can see God at night in the wind and rain. I see creation just about everywhere. The highest form of song is prayer. King David's, Solomon's, the wailing of a coyote, the rumble of the earth. It must be wonderful to be God." (Now, *there's* an original approach!) "There's so much going on out there that you can't get to it all. It would take longer than forever."

It's a message he takes with him everywhere — singing the same kind of songs to the same size (always giant) audiences in London, or Paris or Los Angeles.

It can be old hits like "Mr Tambourine Man" or new ones like "What Can I Do For You?" As far as the fans are concerned all he has to do is sing. Dylan may be best known for his protest songs, but to his audiences protest is only relevant when they can't get tickets for his shows. Yet the protest label sticks — whether he is protesting against war or simply showing that he is angry about anger.

"Being a musician means getting to the depths of where you are," he has said. "And 'most any musicians would try anything to get to those depths, because playing music is an immediate thing. As opposed to putting paint on a canvas which is a calculated thing."

Other people, of course, will say that he simply thinks too much. Music is to be listened to. Not for indulging in a psychological argument. He will challenge that as well.

His music isn't like that of the Great Composers — of either the classics or the lighter stuff. "I don't write every day. I'd like

to, but I can't." No, he claims to be a "total misfit" –
"Gershwin, Bacharach. Those people. They've got songwriting down. I don't really care if I write."

He is, he says, "someone who doesn't comprehend the
values most people operate under. Greed and lust I can
understand. But I can't understand the values of definition and
confinement. Definition destroys."

He wrote his protest songs because he cares. And yet ... and
yet ... They have taken on a totally new meaning to him now.
"I sing 'Blowin' in the Wind' and it seems like an old folk song.
I never think that I have written it myself.'"

He says that what he does now is "Rag Rock" – which is as
good a way of having your musical cake and playing it as any I
know.

Woody Allen
(born 1935)

Woody Allen

Alias Stewart Konigsberg

Would Woody Allen have achieved half his success had he remained Stewart Konigsberg?

For an answer to that question, one needs to know the circumstances surrounding his name change. It came when he was polishing a career on the nightclub circuits, following Mort Sahl's footsteps but at the same time developing style, that prerequisite to success in life. In place of the bitter antagonistic, foulmouthed Sahlisms, came a stream of autobiographical stories that were so funny people came to believe them.

How could you not take to a young man who said his family were so poor they couldn't buy him a dog, but gave him an ant instead?

In the early 1960s that was Stewart Konigsberg, an ant pretending to be a dog with a new name which he figured, probably correctly, would sit better on a nightclub easel.

It was Woody Allen, not Stewart Konigsberg who was spotted by producer Charles K. Feldman, who fits nicely into the story of Jewish show business – and actress Shirley Mac-Laine who doesn't – at the Blue Angel nightclub and invited to come to Hollywood. The result was that he wrote the script for the Peter Sellers/Peter O'Toole film *What's New Pussycat?* And everything else followed on. But this is simplifying a story and jumping a whole battery of guns.

In fact, Woody Allen was born when Stewart Konigsberg was fifteen. It was 1950 and nobody with a name like his had a decent job in the sort of show business he was aiming for.

He used the Allen name when he supplied one liners to Earl Wilson and the other Broadway gossip columnists, causing a great deal of pride to flutter in the bosoms of Martin and Nettie Konigsberg in their Orthodox, observant home in the Flatbush section of Brooklyn – a breeding ground if ever there were one for the kind of Jewish humour that their son has been peddling ever since.

(It could also be argued that it was a breeding ground for the kind of neuroses that keep that other heavily Jewish-populated profession of psychiatrists going in the comfort to which they have become accustomed.)

He saw and he observed – and without necessarily using much of the Yiddish language, transferred a heritage of Yiddish-style humour to outside the ghetto walls. Perhaps for the first time in living memory, the jokes that previously might only have been appreciated in the Yiddish theatres of Second Avenue and Commercial Road are now being told in Hong Kong and Hanover.

From the very start, he showed that he was master of what Yiddishists would recognise as the *sheina galechter*, the bitter-sweet, sad story told against oneself, with more than a splattering of idiotic philosophy thrown in – first in the night-clubs, then on radio, then in the cinema.

There is no better example of this than his marvellous spoof of the great Russian novel, *Love and Death*. Sex and death, he said, were much the same sort of experience. Of the two, perhaps death was to be preferred "because you don't feel nauseous after it".

It was as a writer that he began and it is as a writer that he has continued, although merging writing into performing more successfully than anyone of his generation – perhaps better than anyone since the very different Noel Coward; to say nothing of Chaplin whom in style he somewhat resembles. Chaplin was the tramp who made every movement of his baggy trousers and twitch of his cane into a dance. People laughed as they cried at his misfortunes.

But no, he isn't Chaplin any more than he is Coward. He is very much himself. Perhaps, though, there is also something vaguely Marxist about him – Groucho Marxist, although without the sometimes sadistic wordplay that had Marx Brothers fans rolling in the aisles.

Like Marx he always plays the same character. Like Marx, he looks as if he needs both a good barber and tailor. Like Marx, he talks to the audience. And like Marx he nearly always bombards the same woman with his crazy ideas. The difference is that Marx had Margaret Dumont, a fleshy matron who did little more than puff and blow. For most of his films, Allen has had Diane Keaton, with a shapely figure, a beautiful face and the ability to execute the most complicated dialogue.

She helped to complete his image – the lost, tousled little boy in glasses whom young beautiful women wanted to take to their souls. His trouble was that he wanted them to take him to their beds, and when they did was always worried about his own performance.

Allen is the classic *nebbish* for whom everything must go wrong. He's been described as the cinema's *schlemeil* which isn't so at all; he's far too clever for that.

As early as 1961, he was earning $1,700 a week (translate that into 1980s values) writing for the American Garry Moore Show. Within months of deciding that he could tell his gags better than anyone else, he received what is perhaps the supreme accolade of a performer – an invitation to appear on the *Tonight* Show.

He had a small supporting role himself in *What's New Pussycat?* and disliked it so much that he decided that the only way he was going to do better in the movies was by becoming a director – and acting, too.

His first venture was *What's Up Tiger Lily?* which was based on a Japanese film scenario intended for the kind of people Allen was going to make his career out of playing.

He has not directed all his own films. Nor has he acted in all the screenplays he has written. *Interiors*, a story of a broken middle-aged marriage, not only lacked Allen as an actor. It didn't even have any laughs. But that can be seen as a temporary – if highly artistic – aberration.

The acting bug bit like the jaws of hungry guests at a barmitzvah. He took it to Broadway, too — where in 1966, *Don't Drink the Water,* his play about a Jewish caterer caught behind the Iron Curtain, had been a sensation — and starred in his own *Play It Again, Sam.*

The formula was fixed, and *Play It Again, Sam* about a *Casablanca* fanatic's failed marriage, set the pattern for the movies that were to come — including a filmed version of the play.

The Jewish element remained in all his pictures up and until his 1982 *A Midsummer Night's Sex Comedy.*

In *Take the Money and Run,* he plays someone who can't even learn the tricks of the convict trade. After having failed as a bank robber (the tellers inform him that his threatening note isn't grammatical), he plans a break-out in the prison chapel — a place so strange to him that he shakes backwards and forwards at Mass as though a Chassid in a synagogue.

As the main character in *Annie Hall,* he actually sees himself dressed in the Chassidic kaftan, beard and *streimel* hat, sitting at table with the so-very WASP Diane Keaton's family.

One of the classic scenes in *Play It Again, Sam* shows him

buying Jewish memorial candles – *yahrtzeit* lights – for a dinner party.

It may be that he sees his Jewish roots as connected with the insecurity he displays in all his characters – the Cuban rebel in *Bananas*, the man frozen for two centuries in *Sleeper* (who engages the services of two very Jewish tailor robots), the inadequate in *Everything You Always Wanted to Know About Sex but Were Afraid to Ask* and in *Manhattan*.

It's all in the blood – going back to the time when he first went to a theatre in Flatbush. "I saw every comic, every tap dancer, every magician, every kind of singer. I heard 'Sorrento' sung more times than anyone. I could do everybody's act. I used to tear up the boxes of raisins and write jokes down on them."

He once described his philosophy: "I never think of myself as intellectual in any way and when left to my own devices, which is most of the time, I'm real happy just sitting home, watching baseball on TV and not reading too much. I regard myself as an American comedian in the traditional sense, doing jokes about trying to get pretty women into bed, running away from people who are stronger than me and being cowardly and miserly."

Could anyone not born Stewart Konigsberg have written: "On my wedding night my wife stopped in the middle of everything to give me a standing ovation?"

Which is exactly what people have been doing ever since they first saw him on the screen.

He's found himself a nice job for a Jewish boy.